THE KEY TO DEEP CHANGE

EXPERIENCING
SPIRITUAL TRANSFORMATION
BY FACING
UNFINISHED BUSINESS

DR. STEVE SMITH

In frank, non-technical language, Smith outlines and demonstrates a process for personal transformation—"getting rid of the junk in your life and finding healing for your painful wounds." Beyond attempting to fix symptoms, *The Key to Deep Change: Experiencing Spiritual Transformation by Facing Unfinished Business* uncovers root causes and shows how deep change really happens. Herein you'll find wisdom beyond what many professional therapists have to offer.

Pam: As I mentor younger women, one of the hardest concepts for them to grasp is the reality that God meets us in the middle of our pain and transforms us as He takes us through it. As Steve Smith says, "I don't fix myself. I yield myself to God so that he can fix me." *The Key to Deep Change: Experiencing Spiritual Transformation by Facing Unfinished Business* addresses the two dilemmas all Christians face: "How do I heal from the deep hurts in my life?" and "How do I get freedom from my bondage to sin?" The information in this book is a valuable aid for life change as it connects these two issues, acknowledging in the process that real transformation is only found in a deepening experience with God.

Bob: Smith traces the connections between symptoms, hurts and "sin in me" (Rom. 7:17), along with the destructive results of pursuing false comforts. Well written and self-disclosing, *The Key to Deep Change: Experiencing Spiritual Transformation by Facing Unfinished Business* quickly gets personal. You will find yourself—your hurts, your untamable behaviors, your "stuckness"—in these pages. With these you will find hope for durable change that goes all the way through the heart to bring peace, rest, freedom, and confidence. Following the Christ-centered process Smith outlines, we have seen God change entire families as they allowed Jesus to heal their hearts and break their destructive patterns.

Bob & Pam Putman
Converge Worldwide
CrossPointe Church, Orlando

I cannot express the joy that is found in leading others into transformational healing. After years of very minimal effectiveness in my pastoral counseling, I realized that problems can't be solved without knowing or identifying the real issues. The material in this book has given me a Biblical philosophy and system to lead hurting people out of lifelong woundedness into life giving healing through a transparent love relationship with the Healer.

John Wright, Pastor
Crosswalk Community Church, Titusville, FL

Sola Gloria Deo

Dedicated to my life partner, Shirley, who was with me when the journey was dark and loved me all the while. What a gift from God she has been to me.

TABLE OF CONTENTS

FOREWORD

It was on a ministry trip navigating through the winding back roads on the Island of St. Croix (USVI) when I was confronted with a gut check question from my coach and mentor, Dr. Steve Smith. The question went like this: "Phil, is your preaching transformation based or is it more of an obedience model?" At that moment I tried to cover up my ignorance by giving the best answer I could. After conducting a quick review of past sermons, I had to admit that I was married to an obedience model style of preaching and treatment of others. That singular question catapulted me into a new journey for my personal walk and ministry. I discovered that the process of transformation is more of a cooperative work with God than a self-willed endeavor.

The average church-goer is unfamiliar with the term *spiritual transformation* because for most of their Christian experience, they have been asked to work on obedience and performance. For the past 15 plus years, Dr. Smith has invested his life in teaching the freeing concepts shared in this book to all in his sphere of influence. This book answers a fundamental question everyone must wrestle with: "Do you want to get well?"

In this timely, informative and inspirational work, my dear friend and colleague Dr. Steve Smith provides a roadmap to wholeness complete with turn-by-turn directions carefully drawn from God's word. The lessons depicted in the following pages provide much needed hope that you too can be delivered from the vicious grip of past mistakes and failures, as well as current sins and addictions, as you learn to experience healing from the hand of the Great Physician, Jesus Christ, through pursuing a consistently growing intimacy with God.

Dr. Mercidieu "Phil" Phillips
Senior pastor/teacher (Agape Christian Fellowship)

INTRODUCTION

"As you read...you can expect to have some difficult memories triggered, to have repressed and suppressed long-standing issues and concerns emerge into awareness, and to recognize unfinished business."
Nina W. Brown, Ed.D., LPC:
Children of the Self-Absorbed[1]

Do you struggle secretly—or not so secretly—with inside stuff? Did you expect when you came to faith that you would get rid of all the junk in your life? That all your painful wounds would be healed by now? And yet, are you still wrestling with unholy junk under the surface? Are you angry? Or caught in a growing sense of lust for sexual pleasures which in one part of your brain you know would destroy your life? —Or, are you watching the march of an addiction as it is taking deeper control of your life? On top of all this, have you found that your church attendance is not helping? Perhaps you feel cheated. Or guilty. You feel useless and suspect people at your church think you are useless, too. Perhaps you have tried to deal with all this stuff which I call "unfinished business" but have resigned yourself that it's just not gonna happen anytime soon, if ever.

I had a lot of unfinished business by the time I grew up, even though I was brought up in the church. I did not have the language to explain this then, but I knew I had a lot to hide. And some of it wasn't so out of sight as I would have liked. Speaking as a long-time follower of Jesus, time and religious practice did not change me inwardly. Don't get me wrong, I was outwardly on task, good enough in my faith to go off to Bible college and prepare for vocational ministry. I just wasn't good enough. What I did not know how to fix by effort I did my best to camouflage. And so conflicted I went into ministry with my unfinished business tucked into the recesses of my soul, just waiting to pop out and further damage me and others around me.

It took two years of being in vocational ministry for God to bring me to the end of my self-deception. Can you imagine what a mess I was in, trying to teach people how to follow Jesus faithfully all the while I was in the throes of my growing addictions and personally running from the only One who could heal me? Sounds crazy to me too! But there came a day when I prayed a prayer that went something like this, "God, my life is a mess and if you do not take over, nothing eternal will ever come out of it—in my marriage, my parenting or in my ministry." Since that never to be forgotten day in 1984, God has been guiding me through His transformational process, freeing me progressively from my unfinished business— sometimes willingly, sometimes kicking and screaming! I am still on that journey.

This is a book of challenge and journey. I offer no

instantaneous learning, but I do offer you hope. Hope that you will be changed deeply. Hope that you will be released from what has bound you in life. In this book, I am sharing the transformational lessons learned from my own journey with God so far. But this is not about me, it about us. We all are on the same journey. There is zero difference between you and me. You may have made different choices than I did, suffered different wounds than I did, but the end result has been the same. All of our lives have been damaged and without the transformational work of God, we are toast. No other way exists to become fully human as we were created to be. No way to shed our secrets without ongoing shame and guilt is open to us. I invite you to explore and find hope for your journey also.

Who is this book for anyway? It is not a technical book written for the professional. Instead, I trust you will find that it speaks to you, whatever your place in the church. If you are a:

Church Member, you will find it was written so that you could read and understand its application to your life. People do not experience spiritual crisis for the same reasons, but the pathway out of spiritual crisis is the same for all. The progression of ideas will offer clear guidance for your personal journey.

Lay Counselor, it will give you tools. It is said that the reason people do not offer spiritual counsel to a troubled co-follower is because they do not know what to say. This book offers tools to laypeople who want to truly guide people towards spiritual transformation. You will discover through using the information in this book that you can help people in recovering spiritual health long before they crash and burn and end up leaving the church.

Church Leader, you will find answers to why people in your congregation are stuck spiritually. This book offers insight into the why and how your church can develop a process for helping people move forward again.

Pastor or Staff Person, this book offers you insight for giving spiritual counsel. Most of us in vocational ministry were not trained as counselors, but find ourselves in demand for this service. Most of the Christian counseling books on the market by nature stray in one of two directions. Either the books center on the woundedness of the counselee or guide the counselor to focus on the sin behind the counselee's life situation. *The Key to Deep Change* offers a third alternative—that there is a connection between these two issues and that healing is not to be found in wise counsel so much as it is found in a deepening experience with God alone.

From one who is with you on this journey,
Steve Smith

1. THE JOURNEY

YOU HAVE UNFINISHED BUSINESS.

Whether it is out where everyone can see it, or buried under layers of an efficient and successful lifestyle, the unfinished business of your inner self continues to make its mark on you until you intentionally choose to see it rooted out. This is always a painful process. If you ignore it, it will continue to terrorize you. But if you face it, it will fight you to the death. Yet this must be done or the unfinished business of your life will do what you secretly fear—bring destruction into your world and even worse still, rob you of becoming the person you were created to be by God.

What exactly is unfinished business? It is simply whatever emotional, mental, and spiritual baggage you continue to carry. It is what traps you into living out your life in unhealthy ways, hiding behind the mask of "I'm okay." Or at the desperate level, "I'll survive." Unfinished business is the monster that lives under our bed, bodies hidden in our cellar, skeletons in our closet, secrets not told. It is the unresolved issues that you avoid dealing with even now—or deny that they still exist in you, as if they are ancient history. These are issues from your past that you have never let anyone touch, including God. You may think about getting healthy, of seeking relief from the pressures unfinished business create in your life, but you never really take the right step to deal with it. By this I mean a choice that will put you into a healing process with God.

Why do people like you and me choose not to become as healthy as we could in our souls? Why do we choose pathways that will end in our being much less than we could be? The unspoken reasons are pain and fear. Whenever what is underneath is exposed, it hurts really bad. Unbearably bad. So much so that you would rather go to the dentist and get a tooth drilled without Novocain than face that pain. And this is the fear: That you will have to repeatedly experience the intense pain that is at the root of your unfinished business. The lie Satan adds is, "Alone."

On top of that fear is the uncertainty of what good it will do to address unfinished business. What if you did deal with it? Would you be better for it? Would it be worth it? If you have ever taken a run at dealing with unfinished business, you may think you know the answer to these questions. You may be saying to yourself as you read this that you *have* tried to act on your inner self issues; that nothing changed, that more pain was the result. It isn't worth it, you have decided. But since you are reading this, let me suggest that you have not quite closed the door on hope.

I was almost forty years old before I understood what I am sharing with you. At forty I was an angry man. Every day I woke up ready to be mad at something or irritated at someone—particularly at my family. Shirley and I had been married eighteen years already by this time. She never knew what would set me off on any given day. Our children experienced the dark side of my tongue regularly. I was harsh and critical of every way that they failed to measure up to my standards.

At that point of my life I had taken a risk. I left a secure situation in Wisconsin that had been highly satisfying to help start something new. My partner in this venture had called me one day out of the blue to invite me to join him. I packed my family up and moved a thousand miles to Lakeland, Florida. But the relationship flew apart almost from the beginning. My partner and I quickly discovered that we did not work well together. My anger mushroomed at the difficulty of the situation. I had put my family's future on the line to help this guy. I felt my partner's choices were endangering us (and he probably thought the same of me!). And I felt I was being left out more and more as he pursued decisions that he believed were best. The final straw came when we sat in a local restaurant while he gave me an assessment of my professional growth needs, a conversation that became very personal in nature.

I blew up. All the anger inside me came to the surface and refused to retreat to a manageable level. Weeks went by and finally out of desperation I went to a counselor who listened to me pour out my frustration for four hours. At the end he sent me on a quest that both surprised me and set me on the journey towards transformation.

REFORMATION OR TRANSFORMATION

There is a difference between change and transformation. Most people are told they need to change, from the time they are old enough to take responsibility for their actions. And so most of us try to change when we are unhappy with some aspect of ourselves. This can be an effective strategy if the change sought is within our reach. For example, we can change our negative attitude towards something, like school or work or a person, by practicing positive thinking techniques. We can learn to like what we do not like. We can discipline ourselves from bad habits if we decide fitting in with the rest of the world outweighs being excluded. These changes are not necessarily easy but can be achieved. These are changes brought about by our will. We make new choices to replace the old ones that have handicapped us. If we practice these relentlessly, we will eventually emerge a changed man or woman.

I am a *Trivial Pursuit* kind of guy with a lot of interesting data stored away in my head. From my teenage years, I found satisfaction in correcting others when they mangled an historical fact. This was annoying to many of my victims, although most never mentioned it. Until one friend took me aside and told me the truth about how my know-it-all practices put barriers between me and others with whom I worked. So using a tongue-biting technique, I gained conscious control of this habit and now (for the most part) save my huge repository of trivia for teaching illustrations instead of correcting others.

This kind of change is called reformation. I became a reformed character. The root of reformation is truth—that the change will bring to us to a better life *if* we will exercise our personal willpower. Emphasis on the "if," because many people live life like the pledge of the Men's Club on the Red Green show: "I am a man and I can change…if I have to…I guess." And I know that under the surface, the essential me was not changed. I still want to correct people when they are wrong! I secretly feel the satisfaction that I know and they don't.

Transformation is different on several counts. Foremost, it is about changing the essential me from what I am to what I am meant to be—my created self. But unlike reformation, its power source comes from outside ourselves. It addresses the parts of us that are unchangeable by the exercise of our personal willpower. For example, I was an angry man. I could, by working at it, control my yelling at my wife. I could go for a walk. I could do something physical like chopping wood to drain off the anger. I could use anger management methods and reroute the anger. But I found that I could not stop being angry. That was beyond my ability to change. I needed power from outside of myself to become a peace-filled man. This is what transformation is about. It is also rooted in this truth: That God has called us into a relationship with Him that will bring us to a better kind of life. But in this case, the power source is the empowered presence of God in my life. A shorthand for the difference between these two is:

Reformation = Truth plus trusting in your own strength to do the truth.

Transformation = Truth plus trusting in God's strength to perform the truth in you.

What I discovered was the problem I thought I had was not the problem. It was the symptom of the problem. My partner was not the source of my anger, he only exposed it. After listening to me for four hours, the counselor said, "Steve, there is no doubt things have been done to you that were off-base. But your anger is far beyond what someone else (read *spiritually and emotionally healthy person*) might feel in the same situation. I believe that God is using your partner as a hammer and chisel to open up your soul for healing." That statement stunned me. He then challenged, "I want you to get alone with God for as long as it takes and ask yourself this question before Him: "God, show me why am I angry." This was not the counsel I had expected. I had never thought about asking God to reveal to me the source of my anger, only asking Him to take it away. But I was so overwhelmed by the anger, I actually made time during the next week to get alone with God.

Addressing unfinished business is about facing whatever the real problem is. When a person is sick the doctor does want to know what the symptoms are so she can diagnose the true illness. The reason most people never deal with their unfinished business is because they have spent their time trying to mend its symptoms and found this a dead end. Fixing symptoms leads to a merry-go-round effect. A person will address one symptom, get it to a passable state, and then move on to the next symptom, then possibly to another. But what often happens next is that this person will find himself back at the starting point with the original symptom again. Around and around you go, because fixing symptoms is not permanent precisely because they are symptoms, not the root problem. This approach keeps you chasing symptoms in a circle but never reaching deep inside to find out the "why?" of your particular symptoms. As Bill Gilliam wryly puts it in *Lifetime Guarantee*: "Your problem is that you don't know what your problem is. You think your problem is your problem, but that's not the problem at all. Your problem is not your problem, and that's your main problem."[2]

So I got alone with God and sat with a notepad and pen in hand. I spent two hours telling God what I thought the problem was, filling a page with my ideas. Then I sat for another four hours, not because God was trying to make it hard for me but because it took me that long to become quiet enough to listen. Finally I wrote down a thought that had not come from me—and I knew. I knew even as I wrote it that this was the problem I had closed my eyes to for many years. I wrote: "All my life I have wanted some man to invest in me as if I were worth something." Here was the pain I did not want to face—that I lacked significance in the eyes of other men and felt that I had been judged worthless as a man. I realized that my reaction to my partner was a boiling over from years of pressing this down. It explained why I had never chosen to reach out to a mentor to help me, since I had expected rejection. It showed me that I chose to hide myself behind anger as a means of hiding what I thought others thought of me. I spoke to God that day, asking Him to be my mentor, to be to me what I possibly could not find in another human. My healing process started that day. In a short time my angry days were gone. Let me hasten to add that the anger did not go away because I made it a project and worked on it vigorously. It went away all by itself as God healed me within of what was really wrong with me.

I cannot now remember what it was like to wake up every day ready to be angry. But before, when I was an angry man, I could not imagine what it would be like not to wake up at peace with the world. I recently shared this saga in a meeting with a group of men who have gotten to know me in recent years. One of them told me with a touch of amazement that he would never have guessed I had been an angry man. That is the power of transformation.

Transformation allows people to experience life the way Jesus spoke about in John 10:10: "I have come that they may have life and have it to the full!" The Greeks had two words for life. *Bios* is about the interval of life – its length and events. We use this word to describe the life history of a person (biography) or in our study of planet life (biology). Some Christians think *bios* is the reward of salvation, in that when they die they get to go to heaven and live forever. Eternal life for them is about the *duration* of life. But in this they are misunderstanding the richness of Jesus' offer.

When eternal life is mentioned in the Bible, the word used is always *zoe*. *Zoe* is about the quality and content of the life God gives. When Jesus offers us life, it is of a different quality than the one we have lived. It is about wholeness and renewal through restored intimacy with God Himself right now, not just some day in heaven. This life is about us being fully human in the way we were created to be—to love and be loved without reservation and to have the power to live in freedom from the brokenness, fear, and controls of our past. This includes the power to deal with the unfinished business which prevents us from fully enjoying that life.

FAILED STRATEGIES

If you think the pursuit of becoming a healthy soul sounds simple, that is because it is. And it is hard at the same time. There is nothing complicated about getting physically healthy as we all know. Just eat healthy food in smaller quantities, exercise regularly, and get plenty of sleep. So how many people do you know that follow such a simple plan? How about yourself? It's hard, isn't it? Dealing with unfinished business is the same. But all who have gone this way have never looked back and wished they had stayed where they were, unhealthy in their souls and with a life full of unpleasant and damaging symptoms.

Did I say it's hard? I meant that it's individually impossible to do transformation. I cannot do it. You cannot do it. None of us in our own strength become what God created us to be. I find that this aspect of transformation frustrates a lot of people. With the proliferation of self-help books on the market, plenty want to believe that, if they need to, they can fix themselves. "All I have to do is be obedient in following these spiritual steps and I will be okay," is how they think.

Perhaps this strategy is the one to which people resort because it looks the most Christian. "Just be obedient. Follow what the Bible says and you will be changed. Submit your unfinished business to God and obey." And that is *almost* right, which is why it is so wrong. Some pretty high-profile Christian leaders have recently crashed and burned, confessing of being unable to stop their destructive behavior. So many have failed that it often causes despair in those who watch them. If they cannot, how can I? This shows the lie of the obedience strategy. Everyone in the Bible who was not a Pharisee must have known they'd never be changed by their ability to obey. In a sense, people who try this approach do so like a kind of twelve-step program. Do the steps (i.e., obey) over and over again and you will not slip back into a destructive life. The obedience model directs you to fight the inner foe by your own strength.

When we are not speaking of unfinished business, we can do pretty well in the obedience realm. We can change and adopt good habits. Performing a number of the religious requirements, such as reading through the Bible in a year or doing a daily quiet time, can be within our reach. We can be obedient in dealing with issues that do not have hooks into our soul and perform in ways that helps us fit into our community. For example, someone might say, "Since I have never used alcohol, I can handle obeying the biblical directive not to become a drunkard hands down. In addition, I have never killed anyone and am not currently planning to, even though there are people in my world who really tick me off. So I have won the obedience game once more."

But here this person runs into the truth about the limits of obedience. Jesus put his finger on this in Matthew 5:21-23. He raises the obedience bar. He reveals that the commandment 'Do not murder' includes the probability that you are murdering people by your anger. Count me among those deserving death row. While I was an angry man I figuratively left dead bodies in my wake all the time. And if that wasn't enough failure, Jesus ends his insightful look at the Law with, 'Be perfect as your heavenly Father is perfect' (Matthew 5:48). How will you and I ever achieve that by the obedience model? The pathway God sets out for dealing with our innermost issues is rooted in His power, not our best efforts to obey.

Obedience is the *byproduct* and not the *pathway* to wholeness.

People find that it is hard to accept that they do not have it in them to transform themselves. Depending on God to deal with one's spiritual, mental, or emotional baggage and to bring an end to the resulting symptoms goes against the grain. All humans at some level believe they should be able to be obedient if they try hard enough. So Jesus' words can fall on ears prone to denial.

But what is at stake? Deep change. Deep change brought about by God in who you are so that the inner desires that guide you in your life choices are altered. Deep change that alters your character. This is more than any mere behavioral adjustment that would make you more acceptable in your personal community. Deep change moves you towards the person you were created to be. Deep change is not about what you should do, but about what you will become. It is not "I should be more loving, so I will discipline myself into lovingness." Instead, it is "I want to become the loving person I was made to be and am not yet." You want deep change, which is both available and elusive, simple and hard, whether you are conscious of it or not.

What are your symptoms? Perhaps you are not angry, but are caught up in pornography, wanting it and hating it at the same time. You read erotic romance novels by the bin full and wonder why your marriage lacks that kind of spark. Or whenever you travel, you get an adult movie piped into your room and secretly wish you could sleep with the kind of men or women you see, without guilt. Or maybe it is sex with a child you want, and you are anxious no one finds out as you surf the web for a victim.

Your marriage has gone south, not for the first time. Maybe you're thinking about leaving. You just cannot find the right mate to live with, nor is the person you live with now going to work out long term. You comfort yourself by saying it's not really your fault, but you are lonelier now than ever. Or maybe you have given up on marriage and are putting all your hope in your children. Except they are becoming unruly and rebellious. You wish you could just move away. Or maybe you decided you are going to tough it out, because it is the morally right thing to do. But you hate it.

Your success in business has made it possible for you to live the good life. Funding your dreams is a reality. But you find you have no time for your dreams except now and then— and mostly in the line of duty. You feel drained of energy. That dream home of yours is a place to crash, not live. You think of chucking it all for a slower life pace, but you're not that desperate yet.

Your self-talk consists of words like "stupid" or "worthless" or "ugly" or "hopeless." You have come to the conclusion that no one is ever going to like you because of the way you are, including yourself. You have tried all the self-improvement books and seminars. But nothing has changed.

You still hate yourself. And you are convinced you cannot change. Perhaps you are even thinking you should just kill yourself.

Did you see yourself in this catalog of symptoms? If not, there are more. Whatever your personal symptoms are, however, they are not your problem. They are the display of the unfinished business of your life. So what is the root cause of your unfinished business? That is what this book is going to help you to explore. This is not a counseling manual trying to give you the insights any professional counselor might give. I suspect that if you have already tried that road you may have come away frustrated. Neither is it an autobiographical solution: "How Steve got a healthy soul and you can do the same by following his plan!" No one's journey to a healthy soul can be exactly the same, because we all arrived at our unfinished business by different paths. We have different issues to deal with. But there is similarity to the way out.

Nor is this a how-to-do-a-twelve-step kind of a book, simply because that approach suggests the answer for you is turning yourself into a self-help project. This kind of book is for those who can be ruthlessly honest that they do not have it in themselves to deal with their unfinished business alone.

Possibly you have already adopted a strategy you think is dealing with your unfinished business. I wish you well. But I know that unless your plan is to pursue transformation through intimacy with God, you are not seeing the freedom you thought your strategy would bring you. Let me touch on several common tactics that give the appearance of being engaged in pursuing health, but never set people free. Consider these in light of your personal approach to your unfinished business.

Repression: Some people decide they will not think about the problem, in the hope the pain will just go away with time. This is the survival option. They chose it because they would not have been able to go on without it. They push the pain into a back closet of their minds and close the door. Repression is the attempt to protect oneself by keeping the problem out of sight, a strategy of self-deception. We decide we will not look at it anymore, that we will defeat it by ignoring it altogether. But a thing repressed does not simply go away; it merely takes up a deeper residence within our souls and continues to influence our personal story all the while we are thinking about something else. Furthermore, repression of a problem blocks us from allowing God's love to address the root of what really ails us. If the problem doesn't exist, we will not engage with God about it. This strategy says, "I have no problem."

Lateral moves: Maybe you deal with your unfinished business by making lateral moves, seeking relief in change. Lateral moves are sideways changes we make in place of dealing with the root problem. You may have changed your friends, your job, or the city you live in. Perhaps you changed your lifestyle, found new activities to fill up your free time, changed your clothing style, or changed churches. Maybe you have invested in nip and tuck thinking a younger looking you will bring the contentment you seek. Or changed life partners, thinking your "ex" is the reason for your unhappiness. This tactic of change comes in many different forms, but it always amounts to the same thing—making external changes without inner transformation. You are like the person at a crowded Walmart checkout at Christmas, moving from one line to another in the hope that *this* line will be faster and less frustrating. A forlorn hope. Whatever lateral move you choose, it is really about trying to run from whatever you do not want to face in yourself.

Addressing unfinished business is not about changing the window dressing, but about deep transformation. This strategy says, "Changing something will bring relief." And in a perverse way, change does bring an emotional release, sometimes in a big way. But relief from making lateral moves has a short shelf life. That new relationship or job or electronic toy will not retain its impact of emotional wellbeing. Whatever change you choose is merely a surface bandage over inner unrest. In time, you will find *wherever you go, there you are—* still with the same unfinished business.

Blame game: Victimization is the oldest game in the book. At the heart of this strategy is the resonance of truth. Since you live in a world affected by the Fall, you have been wounded. That is the direct outcome of humanity's rebellion against God's reign. Humans turned on each other.

Unsurprisingly we are the casualty of other people's actions, words, or neglect. Often the wounds come from people closest to you, people whose love for you failed at a crucial moment or perhaps constantly, outrageously, unforgivably. Or maybe for you, like Adam, it was God's fault. No matter who, the cause of your unfinished business is someone's fault and you want them to take the responsibility to fix it if it is going to be addressed at all. It is easy to understand why people choose to develop a blame plan. Yet the tactic fails to deliver real peace simply because you fail to take responsibility for the destructive choices you made, consciously or unconsciously, to comfort yourself in your pain. Pointing at others keeps you from looking deeper inside and owning your own part of your unfinished business. This strategy says, "Someone is going to pay for my pain."

What is the futility of using one of these strategies? These failed strategies fail to bring long-lasting transformation because they are about you trying to self-manage your unfinished business. But unfinished business is about what we cannot really manage in our inner selves. You may have a strategy you think is working for you—ignoring, fighting, fleeing, covering up, giving up—but you start recovering when you finally see your efforts are useless. You may have been at it a long time and have convinced yourself nothing is really the matter, but to be a competent addict you have to be a good liar. Addicts lie to themselves that they are all right, that they are not addicted, that they can conquer this thing when in fact they are in a spiral towards destruction. This is the same for unfinished business.

SURRENDERING TO THE PROCESS

Dealing with unfinished business depends on your surrender to God's reign over you. Not some god or higher power you make up for yourself. This is about the real God who powerfully raised Jesus from the dead to heal your soul. In the first chapter of Ephesians, Paul claims the fullness of God's power used to bring Jesus back from the dead is an available resource for all of His people.

You will never make your soul healthy on your own. Trying hard to reform is not going to work. God did not send Jesus into the world to help us try to change. Jesus came to take over the reins of our lives and to give us his life in exchange. I don't fix myself. I yield myself to God so that He can fix me. I don't try to do the truth; I trust that He is going to do it through me and by His power I take faith steps in response. This is transformation. Not reformation.

But more important, it's about a living relationship with God. One that grows and transforms as you grow and are transformed. No one changes deeply without knowing God better. Without knowing God better, no one sees him- or herself clearly enough to submit to deep change.

I have not finished my transformational process yet. I have

miles to go before I am home. This is a lifelong pursuit. There is always unfinished business. My list of inner issues that affect my real self is probably longer than I thought when I started. Sometimes I don't want to know. Yikes! But this is not a matter of despair for me anymore. God has already brought me a long way down the journey to becoming whole, and I am more confident in Him than in me. He will complete what He has begun in me even when I don't feel like following along after His lead.

Why should you do this? Let's be straight. You will not deal with your unfinished business because I suggest it is the right thing to do. You have stuffed these issues for so long that putting them on the table feels like too much work to you. Nor will you pursue it because of what I have shared about what God did in me. Frankly, your internal emotional resistance to this process may be so great that any half-hearted, misguided start would scare you off before you really engaged with God. I have watched this happen when I taught on unfinished business at my church. I know a man who has run from spiritual health for years. He is an angry man like I was. He terrorized his wife and children. He knew he was troubled. I knew why he was troubled. But he avoided the class like it was fire and he was paper. Finally, a friend who cared about him made him come and came with him every time. The man sat through all thirteen weeks with a blank look, and as much as we loved him, he never did let God into the deep recesses of his soul, causing further sorrow to many who loved him, including himself.

In the end, you only choose to address unfinished business because you are ready to surrender your right to hide behind the someone you were not made to be. You now want to become the created self God made you to be. It does not have to be a decision made out of desperation or crisis, although it may. You may choose to do so because it makes sense, because you want God and what He promises more than you want to live in the grips of a lie.

Why should you do this? Without a doubt the supreme reason is so you will discover a relationship with God you have only read about or seen in others. All our deepest desires and need for security in this world are fully met in being with God, but we only see this to be true as we grow to know Him better and better.

Why should you do this? So you can grab hold of the joy and freedom of *zoe*. You only have been given one life to live. Why waste it? Why not live it to the fullest the way Jesus promised you could? It is for freedom's sake that Jesus set you free (Galatians 5:1). Jesus gave you freedom not just from death, but also freedom from the baggage that unfinished business has produced in you. Why not drop the burden of denial and revel in the loss of shame and false guilt that has haunted you across the years?

This mentioned loss is so necessary for our wellbeing. Nothing robs us of our assurance of the security that we belong to God more than unfinished business. It is the festering sore that infects our soul with shame and false guilt, doubting us into believing not even God cares. And if He does care, He cannot help. It is this robbery of confidence in God that turns us from intentionally pursuing our only hope. We find ourselves wondering whether there really is a God at all. The result is that we lose our way—perhaps never to regain our desire to know God. If we do go to church it won't be because God is meaningful. It just represents a facet of our compartmentalized life, a social group to which we belong. We may still attend church to find a moral anchor, but not *life*. And morality is such a miserable substitute for *zoe*. Maybe as you read this, you catch a glimpse of yourself. Listen, life is hard enough without being held hostage by damaged emotions. Only a confident follower is free from the paralyzing lies that steal joy, limit personal growth, and estrange us from God.

Here's the deal. If you have gained any hope through what you have read so far, why not risk going on? It doesn't take discipline to do this. It takes *courage*. I say courage because you must be willing to submit to God's ruthless searching in the hidden places of your soul. Like David, you will need to say, "Search me, Oh God, and know my heart; test me and know my anxious thought. See if there is any offensive way in me, and lead me in the way everlasting" (Psalm 139:23-24). Ask yourself, "Do I want to be on a journey to wholeness and maturity? Am I willing to accept the challenges that will be necessary to get there? Do I really want the kind of relationship with God that will bring this about?"

How do you start? Here are a few affirmations that you must grab hold of as you begin this ongoing process of letting Jesus explore and heal the hidden recesses of your soul.

First, affirm God's purpose for your life. God is in the process of conforming you into the image of His Son, Jesus (Romans 8:29). So you are not just traveling to the plateau of being good enough. You are on a journey to be changed into His likeness.

Second, affirm that God is using all that happened to you as a part of this process, even the bad stuff (Romans 8:28). This is not just the tragedies and triumphs in your current life, but includes all that has happened to you since the day you were born, even the parts you do not want to remember.

Third, affirm that God is love and that nothing hidden in your life puts Him off or will keep Him from completing His purpose for your life (Ephesians 3:17-19).

Fourth, affirm that God put you into a faith community for this very reason (Galatians 6:1-2). You will need others to join with you in this pursuit, because secrecy gives power to the enemy's lies.

Let me show you the journey you will travel—although not alone.

2. THE STARTING POINT

YOUR JOURNEY STARTS WITH THE TRUTH.

If you are serious about wanting to become a healthy soul, then the starting point of that journey is truth. Not just about yourself. This truth is about what it means to live in the world we have damaged, where in the process we have damaged ourselves. And more essentially, it is the truth about how God has acted to reverse the effects of this damage on you and me.

THE GARDEN STORY

Truth begins with the Garden story found in Genesis 2-3. If you grew up in a church family, you probably first heard this one as a kid in Sunday school. The familiarity of the story can mask its greatest revelations about us as humans. It's about Adam and Eve being created and placed in a perfect place called Eden (which means "delight"), in a perfect relationship with each other, nature and God. The only boundary given to them is not to eat from one certain tree. A serpent appeared, who encouraged Eve to eat forbidden fruit. Seeing the appeal of the fruit, she munched some down and then gave some more to the man for his lunch. After they both ate the fruit, they immediately found the need for clothes. Judgment from God follows for that rebellion, resulting in the first human pair getting kicked out of the garden with curses all around for the man, woman, and snake. Problems galore followed. Those are the basic facts.

Take a closer, more adult look at this event. The story captures the most essential aspects of what is wrong with us. When God created Adam, then Eve, he gave them freedom to do and say all that came into their minds. The relationship between God and the human pair was open and clear. Every day they experienced close community with God. Nothing was hidden between them. In fact, the most crucial part of this story revolves around breaking this relationship.

So what was the big deal of the story? God told them they were not allowed to eat fruit off the Tree of the Knowledge of Good and Evil. If they did, they would really die. The serpent, who is Satan, came to Eve and said in effect, "God lied to you, you won't really die." This is the first time we run into the lies of Satan—lies with which all people will come to struggle. It was a new kind of an idea that the woman had never run into before—that the God she and Adam were intimate with daily might have a double-dealing agenda. It invited judgment by the created on the Creator for the first, but not last, time.

The lie did not stop there. Satan went on with the lie that if they would eat of the Tree of the Knowledge of Good and Evil, they would be gods themselves. Then they could make the right life decisions for themselves without referencing God. *They* could be their own boss. They would know what's right and wrong for themselves. That's what they got when they ate. They actually got the knowledge of good and evil. But personal godhood did not work out the way they thought it would.

The same can be said for all of us. We live every day with the idea that we are in charge of ourselves. That we are making the right decisions for our lives, whether about school, friends, love, marriage, work, etc. Except, like the first pair, our decisions don't seem to work out in the end the way we thought they would. Like God, we have the knowledge of good and evil—but we are not infinite the way He is. So our view of our choices is limited and often shortsighted. We cannot see the damage coming from our choices, or the impact of others' choices who, like us, believe they are making the right decisions for themselves. Damaging collisions between the choices of multiple beings abound.

There was great psyche damage at the moment Adam and Eve chose their own path. None of us can imagine the internal impact of this effect because we live on the other side of the loss of innocence. But up to actually eating the fruit, Adam and Eve were entirely transparent to each other, as indicated by the note in Genesis 2:25: they were naked and felt no shame. This was not just about nudity. Pornography demonstrates that people have the brazen ability to overcome any shame in displaying their nakedness. No, this was about being at complete peace with whom and what they were. Nothing to hide. Nothing to explain. Nothing to regret. It was desire in the best sense of the word—the uncomplicated desire to be totally open to the other.

This immediately changed when they ate the fruit. Before they had no barriers between them. Forever after they felt the need to cover up and hide. Shame became the watchword of all relationships. This was quickly confirmed when God showed up. They hid in the Garden, as if that could actually work. The first recorded words of mankind were, "I heard you coming and I was afraid because I was naked." In this one decision, fear of being seen (that is, known) was introduced to the equation of God and man, man and woman, humankind and nature. This has not changed through the centuries. It is part of the package of the effects from what we call the Fall.

I don't know about you, but of all the friends I have had, I never, not even in my deepest relationships, have experienced a time when one of us wasn't hiding something from the other, when we could not quite reveal all that we wanted to. Why is this issue so important? Because we were created by a unique being whose essence is love. What the Fall did to us was to rob us of our ability to receive love from Him and to give it to each other.

It is a basic human desire to be known without reservation by another. And not just to be known, but to be loved unconditionally by that person no matter what is true about us. Much of our lives turns on this desire. We are out looking for love, whether or not we are conscious of this search. Or despairing of it, for we may have already found that most love is conditional. People will love us if we keep hidden the full truth about ourselves. We cannot be transparent because that will mean rejection. Or the truth about ourselves can be dangerous because it might give someone else power over us. Some of us learned this the hard way. Some know it instinctively.

DOING WHAT WE PLEASE

The greatest effect on humankind out of the Garden debacle was the force of a reality called depravity. Think of depravity as a magnet. A magnet pulls a metal object toward itself. The metal object doesn't have to plan to go, it just does. Depravity is an internal magnet in each of us that pulls us towards damaging choices, whether we really plan to go or not. One man put it this way, "I don't have to, but I can't help myself."

Don't let the word "depravity" put you off. We hear it and immediately think of criminals who commit sadistic acts, those that are the bottom-feeders of society so rotten that extermination may be the only possible way to rid the world of them. What we are thinking about is *utter* depravity. Utter depravity describes the person who has lost all sense of conscience and propriety. It carries a real sense of shamelessness, as the wrongness of their actions can no longer touch their soul.

But the word depravity has a more subtle meaning than just describing people engaged in horrible deeds. In its essential meaning, depravity is just shorthand for doing and choosing what pleases us personally over submitting to God. In short, when I say depravity I am speaking of what I want to do. I choose to do what pleases me. This doesn't mean that I spend all my time doing ugly, destructive things. Depravity implies that I am capable of doing any kind of ugly, destructive action because I am dedicated to pleasing myself instead of God. I can do good things if they please me or engage in bad actions if I prefer. It's my choice. But it does lead me to dangerous and damaging places.

Acting totally for my self-interest is always at the heart of depravity, not good or bad acts in themselves. It is the most basic form of rebellion. If I decide being good, being honest, going to church, not kicking dogs, volunteering time to a homeless shelter, and being kind to my wife is best for me, it is because I chose it. But that does not mean I am a safe person as a result. I could wake up tomorrow and decide, since my desires have changed, that I now want to do just the opposite. The self-interest of depravity means I am not putting any of my life decisions before God to get confirmation and direction.

One of the clearest statements in the Bible for us to grasp on this subject is Jeremiah 17:9 "The heart is deceitful above all things and beyond cure. Who can understand it?" Though we need to understand ourselves, we just cannot seem to get past our self-deception. To move towards a healthy soul we require understanding as to why we're making the decisions we're making. But we don't even recognize that we are acting in rebellion. We think our choices are natural, normal. Others choose what we choose. Why shouldn't we do it? What's wrong with our choices, our way of living? This is the deception Jeremiah is speaking of and it comes from within ourselves.

But you may be doing many destructive things that are actually rooted in the self-interest of depravity. Most people are oblivious to this. To see your choices for what they actually are means you have to have clarity about your life that you currently do not have. The Bible calls this having your mind renewed, a process of letting God change how your mind views the truth of your inner motivations. This awareness is necessary in order to be able to find escape from the grip that depravity has had on you.

Adam and Eve chose what they thought was the right decision for themselves. In turn we inherited this outlook from them. That's why we as their descendants continue to be rebellious. And so we continue to be naturally inclined to do our own thing instead of submitting to what God wants. We prefer what we think we know to what God says. We intuitively assume we can direct our lives, take care of meeting our needs better than God ever could.

What Adam and Eve—and all their descendants—did not realize was that they were actually attaching themselves to idolatry. If God is not the one we will worship and obey, then something or someone will play that role in our lives. These idols we worship are the ones we choose for ourselves—choices that seem to fill us with hope for future pleasure and well-being. These attachments become what we live and die for, even as they fail in their promise. Such is the effect of depravity on our lives. And these attachments play a big part in the unfinished business in our lives.

You may not see this for yourself yet. But your unfinished business, when you decide you are willing to face it, usually has come to the surface because of the pain this idolatry has caused. You may already realize you are not really free in your choices, even as you proclaim such freedom. You don't have to continue in the path you chose, but you can't help yourself. In truth, you have become addicted to what you choose to make the idols of your life, whether they be work, relationships, fantasies, food, spending money, alcohol, recreation, cruelty, or one of an endless host of other things. Your unfinished business is both an inherent part of who you are at this moment, and your worst adversary at the same time. It is robbing you of the Garden—to be truly free and to love and be loved by God and others, without barriers.

As a result of depravity's influence on us, we have restructured the world into a place hard for us to live in. Reflect about this on a global scale. Humankind has collectively created a world full of ecological distress where people live with hunger, poverty, war, and racial strife alongside of technological advances and amazing wealth. With all the best of hopes every generation seeks to find a way to create peace for the world, even as a new form of fanaticism arises and the next dictator is born who will find ready followers. Terrorism stalks the ordinary citizen while the media proclaims continuously about the next pandemic or political disaster or financial depression that is just on the horizon for the comfortable, and is being lived out already by far too many in the world.

While this reality may or may not disturb you personally, the individual impact of depravity is much closer and real to you than what is happening in the rest of the world. You find that certain beliefs you have lived with in comfort are now disturbing your peace and disrupting the peace of your family. This may have been going on for a long time. Or you find you are giving far too much time and unhealthy emotion to specific habits or relationships in your life. New strategies you have tried have not quelled the pain, but have only brought it down to manageable levels for briefer and briefer periods of time. Moreover, people have hurt you—are hurting you—especially those who have a claim on you in some way. Past events of your life, which you have duck taped up and shoved into an internal closet, are now peeking out and clamoring for your attention. You may find your sleep disturbed. The toys you own no longer give you a thrill. Perhaps you just feel empty in some part of your soul. This again is the result of depravity.

The truth we cannot escape is that we have been deeply affected by the Fall, even though we may not acknowledge it. Depravity is not one facet of our life; it colors every aspect of it—all our decisions, hopes, dreams, works, thoughts, and relationships. There is nothing we do or touch that is not permeated by the effects of the Fall.

THE BLAME GAME BEGINS

To deal with the results of your choices you may now be playing the oldest game in the book, namely the blame game. Again we have to go back to the Garden story to find the genesis of this strategy. Adam and Eve eat of the forbidden fruit. The die has now been cast. They change instantly from loving, open partners to uneasy competitors. Then they hear God coming. They hide. When God asks the obvious question, "Why?" Adam firmly owns up that the problem is someone else's fault. In fact, Adam shows an immediate mastery of the blame game. He chooses to put the blame on both God, who gave him Eve as a partner, and Eve herself. God does not stop to debate the point with Adam, but turns to the woman for her view of the situation. She follows Adam's lead. It was the snake who had done it.

This game, as you see, does not need to be taught to anyone. It comes to us naturally. So whose fault is it that you have unfinished business? If you are human you already are blaming someone else, and not without reason. Someone in your world has to be—is!—at fault. It's your dad's, mom's, sister's, brother's, boss's, wife's, husband's, uncle's, pastor's, sergeant's, ex-friend's, teacher's fault that you ended up with these issues. Or like Adam, you blame God. He failed you. He did not protect you. He burdened you with the handicap, problem, hurt, or violation you have lived with and hidden away all these years. Maybe for this reason you have broken off your relationship with Him and any of the others that landed you into this mess.

You can go on blaming God or other people for your life. There is no external mechanism to stop you. No lecture, no commandment, or pressure can be applied by anyone to make you change your mind about who's at fault for your unfinished business. But please understand that you will not only stay stuck in your situation, it will intensify as time passes. Unfinished business is not about the past alone. It is what affects your present and will continue to create havoc in your future. The blame game is a smoke screen keeping your eyes blinded to the way out. All it offers is a false comfort that you are not responsible.

Here's the point you must accept as truth if you are going to go on from here down the healing journey. You must accept that it is you that have made the life choices that make up your unfinished business. That what you have become, for good or ill, is the product of your decisions. You have to own the results instead of rejecting the painful parts as being wholly someone else's creation. David Benner, in *The Gift of Being Yourself*, observed, "You must accept all parts of yourself before you can surrender them to God for healing and transformation."[3] As you will see, accepting this truth plays a large part in identifying how far you will travel towards becoming a healthy soul.

So ask yourself the following questions:

- How have I chosen to live as a result of what others or life has done to me?
- Do I live in fear, defiance, rebellion, addiction, alienation, loneliness, disconnection, and with a goal of proving I am somebody?
- Have I chosen to bury the past and deny the pain as my strategy for moving forward?
- Have I developed habits that I use to mask the pain, even though they were unconsciously acquired?
- Is someone the object of my anger and bitterness?
- Can I even admit to myself that I have made these choices?
- Do I have broken relationships in my life, people I cannot stand to be with due to their part in my pain?

Somewhere in the process of answering these questions, you may take the first move of owning up to the fact that your unfinished business is not just the fault of someone out there. It is the problem you helped create for yourself.

This is unfair, you might think. It is not fair that I have to shoulder the blame for what others did to me. And you would be right. But you are not being counseled to shoulder what others did—but what you did in response. If you think that is unfair, remember that fairness ended at the Garden of Eden.

THE GOOD NEWS

If the Garden story is a tragic one for us, it is also a hope-filled one as well. Had God handed out complete justice, total annihilation would have been the ending. Instead, in a series of judgments we see God revealing His heart. Speaking to the serpent first, God said in effect that conflict would be the way of life between the snake (read Satan) and mankind, but that a descendent of the woman would defeat him even as the snake tried to destroy that offspring. The rest of the Bible is the unfolding of this promise. It is the beginning of the story of mercy and restoration revealed in the death and life of Jesus, God's provision for the way back for all of us who have no claim on His mercy. It is a promise of *sacrificial love*. This truth is also critical for anyone who wants a healthy soul.

What is it that we learn about God's love in this story? First, that God's love is action, not emotion. Our love for a number of people in our lives is limited to what we feel. Our emotions dictate whether we are in love or not. We hope that the person we love feels the same about us and feel sorrow or hurt when our love is not returned. This is not so for God. He *chooses* to love and demonstrates it by actively loving those who really do not care for Him at all. This kind of love is called *agape* in the Bible. It is willful love, a decision to act for the good of those He loves without regard for love being returned. What this part of the story tells us is how deeply God loves those He created. He is the one who sets in motion a way of reconciliation between humanity and Himself, not the other way around. Instead of expecting people to figure out what actions to take to restore their relationship with God, He sets out a plan that will depend solely on Himself to bring it about.

The second feature of God's love found here is that He loves in the face of the most devastating acts of rebellion. Our love for someone might not survive if that person stabbed us in the back with utter disregard for truth and a total lack of concern. Perhaps you know this through personal experience. But God did not respond as people do. And not just with Adam and Eve. God knows the worst about you and me. He sees past the pretty face we put over our broken soul and He persistently loves our created self. Nothing is hidden from Him—not our darkest secrets covered by our most sincere lies. Nothing deters Him from His love for us.

Let me hasten to add that His love will not keep us from the consequences of our choices. Adam and Eve ate the forbidden fruit. They had been told what the results would be, but still they ate. The consequences that followed—the judgments, the loss of Eden as home, and the running down of their life's clock—were no surprises, even though they were sorry that they received them. We are just like them. We make life choices all the time that come with consequences we would rather not live with. Does that stop us? Actually, it is the consequences of our acts that often cause us the most anger at God. We feel they are too hard, too unfair. Since we are sorry we think that it's only fair that they be lifted. But seldom do they go away. And so we stew at God even though we may lie to ourselves that we are not really angry at Him.

There is purpose in the pain of consequences. Those things we have brought on ourselves drive us towards God. We are not being punished by God. The actions we chose had built in penalties, like the one Adam and Eve already knew about before they took the first bite. But it is these very costs that remind us we are the created, not the Creator. We cannot fix what we and others have caused to go wrong. We need someone to rescue us from the mess we have made for ourselves, someone who loves us in spite of the fact we do not love Him.

This leads to the third characteristic of God's love in the Garden story. God is not interested in cheap forgiveness. Cheap forgiveness is the kind that comes from someone who is unwilling to do the hard work of restoration of those who are broken. This kind of person is saying that the damage you have done to yourself does not really matter to me. Cheap forgiveness is the essence of a "faithful and just to forgive" without a "cleansing from all unrighteousness" kind of relationship.

But we do matter to God. He knew the strength of the immense grip that depravity now had on humankind. It was not about how to appease Him on which the story turned. It turned on His decision about how to rescue and restore those He had created from the consequence of their decision. Their very lives were at stake. "I forgive you" would not overturn death. Death as a consequence had to be paid. Its right to the life of every man and woman had to be broken for them to be made whole again. And so He chose to take their consequence on Himself. In doing so He demonstrated not only His love but also His mercy. Rebel as we might, God is willing not only to forgive us but is also committed to restoring us from the damage done to us by our own choices, even though we don't deserve this kind of treatment.

Here is the truth about love. As a human, your deepest desire is to be loved. This is why you are exploring this journey. What you are looking for in life is God. Not just because God is loving but because God is Love. His being defines love, so all His actions towards you are rooted in love. Your needs are driving you towards God, not away from God. The dividing issue between you and God is not the consequences of your choices but who is going to be in charge. If you choose to substitute your passion to run your own life over your greater need for love, every decision you make is really about trying to find love somewhere else or in someone else. Try as you might, when you look for love apart from God, who is the source of love, you will not be heading towards becoming a healthy soul. After all, how can damaged people find health in a world that has been damaged by our choices?

God's active love for you trumps what you may be feeling about yourself at this moment. Perhaps one of the outcomes of your choices is that you have no love for yourself. Behind your mask is the pain of self-hatred, of feeling you are a failure, or worse. While you may not be able to believe this at the moment, God who created you has a better understanding of your value than you do. If He who created you is unfailing in His love for you in spite of all the warts you have developed, how can you do less?

WE HAVE BEEN GIVEN EVERYTHING WE NEED FOR THE JOURNEY

So where is all this leading? I hope you do not believe this is about becoming more religious. Religion at its best is our personal effort in response to God's love. That can be one possible outcome. But it is not a substitute for becoming a healthy soul. I do not know how many people I have worked with who have used religion for a cloak to hide both their unhappiness and unhealthiness. One woman I knew used it as a club to beat up her family members caught in the web of her blame game. A painful truth is that churches are often full of people who have no intention of becoming healthy. Their approach to God actually helps them to maintain a barrier between them and health.

No!—where this is leading is towards a deeper knowing of God and a more profound understanding of God's empowering presence in your life. I assume that if you have already come into a living relationship with Him, you have some grasp of the idea of salvation. You have surrendered your life, asked Jesus to be Savior and Lord of your life, and have hope of going to heaven when you die.

Right now, you may have a bunch of issues overwhelming you. You may feel defeated by the way you live. You may be using camouflage to keep people from seeing these parts of your life. (Religion is one example, but another is being socially outgoing or its opposite—being very private; or being indispensable and handy so no one will ask questions; or controlling people and information; or putting on a happy face. Smokescreens come in numerous forms.) But you know the hidden issues slip out. And if no one else knows, your family does. Moreover, you yourself have a backstage view of yourself. You know the truth. You see no way to fix yourself. The idea of becoming whole seems laughable to you.

Coming to know the depths of God's love for you is essential to have the courage to go on. Failing to believe the truth of this fact is at the center of why you struggle with trusting God with your life.

Perhaps you do find this truth hard to believe. Your inner voice may tell you that God is not all that pleased with you.

One person I know told me that for many years she thought God must be disgusted with her for all the ways she failed to measure up to His standards. You might even think God has it in for you, that He really does not want you to succeed in your life. While I cannot sweep away these lies for you, I can affirm that God's love for you is deeper and more amazing than you can imagine. You will find as you come to know Him better that His love contains the power you need to address your unfinished business.

This is why the gospel is *good news*. God has not made His transformation of you dependent on your own puny strength. Out of His love God has given you everything you need to be saved from the power of sin...everything you need to be transformed...everything you need to address your unfinished business.

This is not something that God will give you later on when you have become a good person. The power to be transformed was gifted to you from the instant God made your spirit alive. Otherwise transformation would be impossible. Note how Peter said in his second letter. "His divine power has given us *everything we need* for life and godliness through our knowledge of Him who called us by His own glory and goodness. Through these He has given us His very great and precious promises, so that through them you may participate in the divine nature and escape the corruption in the world caused by evil desires" (2 Peter 1:3-4). What is he saying? That there is nothing you lack to be made whole from the corruptions in the world. You have been empowered through your connection with God in such a complete way that you no longer have to continue to live being damaged and damaging others. Note that this is based on God's promises, not just on Peter's wishful thinking.

Paul expands on this theme in Titus 2:11-14. "For the grace of God that brings salvation has appeared to all men. It teaches us to say 'No' to ungodliness and worldly passions, and to live self-controlled, upright and godly lives in this present age, while we wait for the blessed hope—the glorious appearing of our great God and Savior, Jesus Christ who gave himself for us to redeem us from all wickedness and to purify for himself a people that are his very own, eager to do what is good." What does this mean for you? It means you are already ready to deal with your unfinished business. The underlying power for this is the grace of God "that brings salvation and teaches us to say, "NO." I'll talk more about grace later on. What you need to see right now is that you have everything you need from God to be made whole. You do not need to wait for something. You don't have to pray for it. You don't have to pay your dues to the Lord. You don't have to read the Bible more. You don't have to wait for someone to come and lay hands on you. God has already given it to you. The issue is that you must appropriate—grab it and use—what God has already given you.

Since you now know the truth—that you have been given power for this journey—let me encourage you to further explore the journey I am describing.

3. WOUNDEDNESS

EVERYONE YOU MEET IS WOUNDED.

Of some people you know this intuitively. They talk about the world in terms of pain and loss. Their life journey is highlighted with hurt and disappointment. In fact, their story focuses on their life wounds. They can relate all the past wrongs and pain that were inflicted on them in detail—and do not hesitate to do this even with strangers. For these people, their hurts have become the center of their lives, so loud in their ears that they cannot hear anyone else's pain.

For others, talking about woundedness is either disturbing or a waste of time. They think, "Yes, people have experienced pain. But talk will not change that. It's better to put the past to rest, to accept what happened and to move on." Many of these people believe time has—or will—heal all wounds. Others in this group have sought to bury their hurts deep, either under layers of achievement or forgetfulness. Still others use Scripture as a band-aid over their wounds, refusing to let the Spirit do a deep cauterizing work in their hearts. They live in the heady land of 'spiritual triumph' where they believe they have been healed without ever acknowledging their wounding or asking God to deal with the mess it left behind. I sometimes wonder what they make of David's anguished psalms.

Woundedness is not about passing hurt feelings that dissipate with time. Nor is it about the kinds of wounds that discipline inflicts, the 'this-will-hurt-for-a-time' sort given by a parent or mentor that ultimately helps you to become more mature. These are the soul-touching kinds of pain that not only do not fade, but continue to bleed years after the wounding.

My wife and I once let a homeless man live with us for almost a year until he could get on his feet. He and I had the same conversation almost every day, one in which he guided us into talking about his divorce. He would speak about how his friend betrayed him and stole his wife. He reveled in the time when he bashed the man in the jaw. He'd weep about his children having to grow up without him. How the agony over the divorce cost him his job, his home and his happiness. When did this happen to him? Ten years before I met him. But inside him it was as fresh as if it had happened the week before last.

Whether we are public or private about our pain, this kind of pain resides in all of us. We may no longer feel the immediacy of it as my friend did, but the pain does more to shape us than we perceive. This woundedness is the origin of your unfinished business. This may be the hardest turn on the journey to face. Why? Because it is here that you will have to look intentionally with God into areas in your soul which you would rather leave alone.

I've learned something from counseling people over the years. What drives most people to ask for help has to do with painful stuff with which they no longer want to live. These usually are outside issues that bother them, such as rebellious children, marital strife, or some kind of addictive behavior. In reality, the pressures that send them for help are normally not the real problem. That issue is the tipping point, the last straw these individuals no longer can bear. Some have to be pushed by friends towards help because they have developed such a strong internal survivalist system over the years. Others come because they need someone's ear, although they are not necessarily committed to taking counsel. Some never come, choosing to tough it out or to self-counsel through books, seminars, and informal advice systems. My practice with those who come to me is to share with them the following Heart Chart as a starting point for understanding how to really address what needs to be addressed.

The area above the top line represents what's going on in their visible life. The middle and bottom spaces are about what is going on inside them.

The starting point of addressing unfinished business and becoming a healthy soul is what is going on in the heart. Unlike the Valentine's Day view that the heart is the seat of the emotions, the biblical idea of the heart is that it is where we make our life choices, where our rational thoughts and emotions are weighed to determine what we will do or become. This is the essential soulish part of us, for here we settle on who we are, what we will do, and how we will present ourselves to the rest of humanity.

Our unfinished business keeps our heart from functioning properly. The wounds we have received by living in a world affected by the Fall have damaged our emotions. As a result, our damaged emotions offer false guidance to our lives. More to the point, our heart's function of making choices is affected by the unhealed wounds we carry within. These unhealed wounds are the *hurt of the heart*. We have accumulated them throughout our lives. Many times they are related and interlocking wounds. We may bury them inside, seeking to become unconscious of their presence, but they do not go away on their own.

ORIGIN OF OUR WOUNDS

Where did this *hurt of the heart* come from? Many

sources. Primarily it comes from living in a world full of people who, like ourselves, are affected by the Fall. Wounds come from people who are supposed to love and protect us, whose love failed at a crucial intersection between them and us. They were not necessarily *seeking* to hurt you; sometimes they were just doing the best job they could of helping you to become a responsible adult. But their preferred choices for your life, made so casually, so unthinkingly, may have cut you deeply. The sad part of this is that they often do not even remember wounding you.

The wounds that come from this source are especially remembered by you, however. I once spoke to a room full of men. When I began talking about having issues with their fathers, every man leaned forward listening intently. This is where many people—not all—start gathering wounds. Perhaps you can relate here. You remember your mom's and dad's failure to be good parents, sometimes by acting unfairly, sometimes neglectfully, sometimes intentionally and brutally. You may have been left with the opinion that you are at fault for your parent's divorce or are the cause of their addictions. Some of you were physically abused. Some were sexually used by adults that you love. Some of you were told you were not wanted. Or that you could never measure up to your parents' expectations—or would always be outshone by your sister's abilities. Or you couldn't go anywhere because you might get dirty or hurt or lost. Maybe told that you were always going to be a failure, a disappointment. Maybe you grew up in an abusive home, an alcoholic home. Maybe your parents were workaholics and you never saw them. You felt abandoned, or emotionally deprived, or mentally abused, or smothered.

And you have not resolved this hurt in a productive way. There are still subjects that you cannot or will not talk about with your parents. You swore when you grew up, you would never be like them. You would do a better job with your kids. Why? Because you think by this you can address the pain you still carry in your heart from your childhood.

I'm never surprised when successful but driven businessmen finally reveal that the root of their drive is found in their childhood. For many, they are trying to prove their worth to their parent, looking for the praise that never comes. Some were told they would never amount to anything. Some are looking for approval from parents long dead.

It is possible that the most serious wounds you carry did not come from your parents. Instead, their source is traumas that have been extremely painful in your life. Maybe your trauma was that somebody you were very close to died tragically. Or people who were close to you let you down or stabbed you in the back. Or maybe because of your personal limitations you were made the focus of other people's comments and contempt. I read of one woman who was extraordinarily beautiful, but could never accept that as true because of the humiliation she carried from teenage acne. Loss, humiliation, exclusion, and deprivation all leave hurt in our heart that we do not outgrow.

Others live hurting over lost opportunities. You missed your chance to go to college. You lost out on the ideal job, which would have met your family's financial needs as well. You did not take the time to call and restore that broken relationship, to say you were sorry. Now the chance is gone to the grave. You messed up. The moment is gone. The person you loved has packed his bags and moved—or married another. For years these wounds will hang around so that you can kick yourself around the block regularly.

We can add another category of wounds—those we inflict on ourselves. Most of these come from bad decisions due to immaturity. The car crash when you were drunk that cost a friend's or family member's life. The bad choice you made to forsake something that really was of great value to you. The wasted school years that now prevent you from pursuing the career path you want. The rebellion you lived out against the structure that dad and mom set up to help you grow up soundly. The bad personal habits you fostered. All these have the potential to drive thorns into your heart that will ache.

There is no time limit on when wounds can be inflicted. As long as you are alive, the potential for deep wounding exists. The story is told of a beloved elderly man, a gentle and respected church leader who many looked to as a role model for how to finish life well—until his wife died tragically. The pain of that loss wrapped around his soul. Before long he had indulged in bottle after bottle of alcoholic forgetfulness, which turned him from a gentle person to a vulgar and violent man. People who had known him for years were shocked and could not grasp why he had let his tragedy change him so much for the worse. But it is never too late in life to be wounded.

I spent years trying to live with pain. I thought I was able to cope pretty well. My approach was to bury it deep and just get on with living. But it would not stay buried. Pain had a way of popping out, not just in sleepless hours of the night, but also in the midst of my work day, my days off, and times when I was with my family. Some reminder would trigger the lock on that part of my soul and out the pain would spring. It disconcerted me when it appeared because I thought I had it firmly under lock and key.

The intensity of some pain can be rechanneled in time. I can work it off by honest labor or volunteering to serve others in pain. Or I can follow a grief process and learn to live with some pain, such as loss through death. I can use denial and convince my observable emotions that it never happened. What we may not understand is the enormous quantity of pain that we are battling. Much of it sneaks past our defenses, if we have any, and takes up residence in our souls while we are distracted by life in other arenas, like the challenge of growing up, going through puberty, learning how to work or to be married, or parent children. Even when we are aware of the hurt of the heart, we often lack a plan or the energy to work the plan to address all the pain we do know about.

You personally may doubt you have wounds with which you are dealing. This is not just a denial technique with you. You really are not aware of anything to be troubled about from your past. Perhaps this is not your time to deal with your wounds. It may be that some day in the future at a time of adjustment, loss, change, crisis, illness, or some tragedy you will recognize the trace of a long forgotten blow, or sense an inner disquiet that will open locked rooms inside you that you did not know even existed. Until then you have to accept that there is something in you buried just beyond your reach at the moment. But understand this—that something is guiding your journey and helping to create your unfinished business.

On the other hand you may be willing to explore something with God that is uncharted in your knowledge. Without demanding a full picture, you can say to God, "Search me, Oh God, and know my heart; test me and know my anxious thoughts. See if there is any offensive way in me and lead me in the way everlasting" (Psalm 139:23-24). In asking this, you are opening yourself to revelation about your soul's symptoms that only God has the ability to show you. This is the *ruthless search prayer*. You are saying to God that you are ready to know what He is willing to show you for the sake of your soul's health.

AVOIDING THE VICTIM MENTALITY

While I do not believe in playing the blame game, in a great many instances there are people responsible for hurting you in ways that were unwarranted and cruel. You might choose to see yourself as a victim. What happened was not your fault, you assert. And you would be right. What people do to hurt others is never okay. Some of their acts were criminal. As a result of what they did you may have spent hours and many dollars getting counseling.

There are many good people who counsel but not all counsel they give is good. Some counseling can actually add to your emotional pain through the advice given. I remember when TV followed one popular counselor who encouraged his counselees to let their inner anger out at those who had hurt them. With plastic baseball bats, people would beat on an empty chair that represented their antagonist, all the time telling the chair how angry they were for the pain inflicted. As was discovered later, the problem with this approach was that no one really was being healed from their pain. It gave them a temporary outlet for their pent-up emotion, but not a restorative journey.

The danger of this kind of counseling is that it encourages you to become attached to being the helpless victim. The idea is to believe everything that came to pass in your life was beyond your control, that you just happened to be in the wrong place at the wrong time. It is right to recognize you are a victim of actions you could not control. But developing a helpless *victim mentality* will always add to your pain. While it is true that people and events have hurt you, you still have a choice about what you are going to do in response to the pain. People immobilized by a victim mentality think they have no role in their continuing pain.

Some of you have endured terrible abuse through no fault of your own (although you may believe somehow it was). You were someone's sexual prey. Or maybe someone made you his or her personal punching bag. Many stories people tell of their abusive past are pure horror. No one who is outside those histories thinks *you caused* people to abuse you, to hate you, to rob you of personal dignity and humanity. No, the issue you have to confront is *what did you do to cope with the wounds?* Where did you go once you were beyond the grasp of the perpetrator? Did you choose to continue to define yourself as one who was used and abused and paint your life choices as natural results of the life you survived? Or did you choose to be strong, yet still in secret the memories ache and the way you are coping is not getting you past the pain?

One person I know coped with the hell of having to live with a cold, abusive grandmother after his father deserted his mother when he was a young teen. He escaped into an emotional cave away from the pain. The result was he carried that survival mechanism into his marriage and it ultimately became a weapon of mass destruction against his wife. You may have chosen to be a clown, or a hero, or a perfect child to deal with the abuse you lived through. The residue of that choice now complicates your life as an adult.

Sometimes people are participants in the hurt that haunts them. I once met a young woman who had spent years of her life in depression. As a teen she had fallen for an older man. He secretly promised her marriage. As he was many years older, their relationship was opposed strongly by her father. To see each other, she would meet secretly with him, sometimes even in her own home when the family was not there. Before long their relationship became physical. But this was okay in her mind because they were going to be married. But then, when she was still a minor, her family moved across the country. Her lover found another bride. She went into a tailspin. It was only years later that she shared with her family the reason for her depression. She saw herself as the victim of this man. She felt she could not move on and pursue a productive life. The family affirmed her victimhood and went looking for his head.

There was no question in my mind that the man had defrauded her. He had dishonored his promises to her and had involved her in sexual sin. All of his actions flouted her father's edict to stay away from his daughter, especially by coming into the father's own house to do the damage. What was worse was that he denied he had made any promise to her, adding rejection to her pile of pain. In all this she was the victim.

Yet look at the decisions she made in the process. She preferred to believe her lover's promises over her father's protection. She made the decision to meet him secretly, even in her own home. She freely gave in to sexual acts that she knew to be wrong outside of marriage. In fact, it was the idea of a victim mentality that allowed her family to place all the blame on her former lover and account none to her. The added denial of her choices in the matter only helped keep her stuck. She chose to view herself as only the victim instead of one of the participants. And it further unraveled her life. Instead of her confession helping her to become healthier emotionally, her lack of ownership sent her into a deeper tailspin, keeping her immobilized for more years as she sought her way out of a labyrinth of her own choices.

Victim mentality is just a maze of wrong beliefs about ourselves and our choices. It suggests that the victim is to be pitied and protected because of the wounding process instead of being challenged to examine and own the journey he or she followed *after* the blow that wounded. It promotes learned helplessness—that the individual is unable to recover without being rescued (if that person is even willing to be) and the perpetrator punished.

In fact, the idea of powerlessness is at the core of victim mentality. We are led to believe we have no power available to address our wounds, unless it is the power to hide or ignore them. This is one of the lies whispered into our ears by the enemy even as we make powerful choices to pursue further entrapment with our wounds. The truth is, all of us can make choices in the face of incredible pain that will lead us to become healthy souls. We are not stuck with taking what is dished out to us, no matter what we are told. But this available power is not generated from within ourselves.

Here is something you need to recognize if you are going to pursue a healthy soul. Your damaged emotions will lie to you. They will let you believe that others, not you, have to own what they have done to you in order for you to get well. We accept these lies because in our hearts we all want to believe we are innocent. That what happens to us is unfair. That life should be good—good in the way it might have been before the Fall—and that if it is not, it never can be our fault. You may hear yourself saying lies like this right now.

One of the other pervasive lies is that you cannot move on and get well until someone *apologizes* for their wrongs to you, whether it be mother, husband, or God. Someone has made you the victim and you cannot go forward until they humbly confess their wrongs and make them right. The lie of required apologies for healing keeps people stuck all their lives, not knowing that dealing with unfinished business never is about what *others* need to do, but what *you choose* to do about your damaged emotions. No one but you stands in the way of getting well. Are you willing to trust this truth enough to move further along on your journey to health?

DAMAGING OUTCOMES

When our heart gets hurt the emotion mechanism in our souls gets damaged. As a result, what I consider as a normal reaction to a situation may really be abnormal. My emotions now operate outside of their normal boundaries and color how I see my world. More than that, these damaged emotions change the way my will functions. To make a wise decision, I need both my rational thinking and my emotions to participate. But when I am making a decision in an area affected by my damaged emotions, they take control of the decision-making process, blocking me from hearing any rational input. This doesn't mean that all the time I am acting abnormally. In many areas I may be sensible and normal, but there are certain areas that are out of rational control.

Think of the will function as a balance scale.

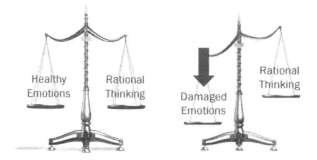

On one side of the scale you place your rational thoughts. On the other you place your emotions. If both are healthy the scale balances out in the decision-making process. But let's say your emotions are damaged—bruised and swollen from the *hurt of the heart*. When they are placed on the scale, the added weight of the painfully bloated emotions pulls the decision in their direction, even if the resultant decision seems absurd or harmful to all those around you.

For example, why do I keep eating when I am way overweight and can no longer fit comfortably into my clothes? My rational mind tries to tell me this is a bad decision, but my damaged emotions override those thoughts, telling me I need this leftover spaghetti, I deserve this ice cream. Or why do I get mad at other people on the road who are in my way when I am the one speeding? My rational mind tells me to slow down but my damaged emotions weigh in with the thought that cursing and taking dangerous chances to pass them are better ideas. If I win against people who are not even trying to compete with me, I feel better. Does this make sense? No, but it is a sure sign my emotions are in charge of my will.

We even say stupid stuff and to our ears it sounds reasonable. Why do we overspend at sales to buy things we really don't need? To save money! Why do people abuse animals through dog- or cock-fighting? Because it is entertaining. Why would I cheat on my wife by taking up with another woman? Because I am in love. Those damaged-emotion responses explain everything. I once had a friend explain to me that he had to have an illegal radar detector in his car because he could not help speeding. Several times I have sat with people who were thinking about committing suicide and heard them explain how killing themselves would be for the good of their families. The term "rationalization" was coined for this very purpose—we are seeking to make our damaged-emotion decisions appear to be rational when they are not.

If we want to recognize this tendency in ourselves, look for the times when we refer to how we *feel* about an issue or a personal relationship. This is the language of emotions guiding our will decisions. Why did we decide to act the way we did? Because of the inner feelings that drive us. We *feel* trapped. We *feel* afraid. We *feel* that person doesn't care for us, is disgusted with us, is bad news. We *feel* leaving our marriage is the right thing to do. We *feel* God Himself doesn't care. We judge the reality of many life situations by how we feel. We know at some level that we shouldn't hate that person, but it is how we feel. We know we need to get out of the house and do something for someone else, but we don't feel like it. The feel of our inner self colors the world in which we live.

We can be trapped in search of wholeness because our damaged emotions force us to focus on the external instead of the internal. We feel like our problem is external. Our problem is our dad, our mom, our kids, our environment, our society, our drinking, or our temper. We feel like these are our real problems. These are lies our emotions are telling us. Somewhere out there we'll find wholeness. We feel this is true instead of recognizing there's something wrong inside of *us*.

Choices based on damaged emotions lead us to use some

form of external *if only*. "*If only* my spouse would just shape up I'd be okay." "*If only* my boss would just keel over and die I'd be okay." "*If only* my children would just move away I'd be so much better off." "*If only* I could just meet the right man." "*If only* I could change the past." These are also emotional lies. Our damaged emotions have created a reality for us that we feel is true. We feel we have no choice! Feeling, rather than truth, is our guide to the right action. Notice in yourself how often you use the word "feel" in your own view of your world.

Another pertinent word in the language of emotions is fear. Since this damage is a result of living in a world affected by the Fall, fear in some form is part of the everyday experience of all of us damaged people. This is one of the guises of collateral damage that comes from being wounded. Fear is not the wound itself. It arises from the dust of the wound. Some of the forms that fear takes include fear of relationship, which may manifest itself in loneliness, alienation by pushing people away, inferiority, inability to trust people, even sabotaging relationships. The fear may be of intimacy. Perversely, another may fear being alone while fearing rejection at the same time. A person may live in fear of the world, people, or events. Hyperactivity can be a product of the fear of being still and quiet, triggering a chemical change within the person's physical make up. Or the same fear may show up as drivenness, leaving the person unable, even unwilling to relax. Others need rigid rules because their fears tell them they will be safer if life is regimented. On and on goes the fear list, revealing insecurity, self-hatred, suppressed emotions, expectations of failure, and confusion. All these fears can be well hidden behind a mask, but the person in the grip of fear often knows his or her particular brand of fear is pulling the strings of life.

We fear, so we learn to hide our damage so that no one will see it and perhaps use it against us. We fear ridicule. We fear more of the same. We fear showing weakness. We fear pity. We fear on many fronts—normal relationships for example. Ask a woman who has been sexually molested about that fear. Right now you are carrying fear inside you, although it might be masked and renamed as something else. Living fearfully is not the issue. There is just no one you trust with the secrets of your soul. And lacking trust to be transparent is what fear really is all about.

A tangible outworking of fear is relationship loss. If you are looking for an indicator of where you might be wounded, think about whom you would never in a million years friend on Facebook. Or invite to your birthday party. Or even let know your new address. Broken relationships litter the ground behind those of us who are running on fear. To protect the wounded part of our souls, we unremittingly guard against those whom we think caused the wounds. Self-protection is the watchword of fear, because we have consciously or unconsciously determined not to open ourselves to more pain.

In addition to fear, collateral damage takes another guise in people's lives. People with unfinished business become hard hearted. Being hard hearted means having a will that chooses to say "No" right in God's face. For a hard hearted person, it does not matter what is healthy, whole or maturing. Instead, he or she twists the facts to line up, however imperfectly, with their preferred outcome. Look at the confrontation Jesus had with the religious leaders over divorce found in Matthew 19:1-12. Inviting Jesus into a divide and conquer discussion, these leaders were looking to see where he would come down on a hot button issue of the day: "Is it lawful for a man to divorce a wife for any reason he can think of or is divorce restricted to a handful of "biblical" reasons." They were pretty sure these were only two possible positions on the matter. Jesus shocks them by telling them God had an utterly different perspective—what God had put together should not be separated by the maneuverings of people affected by the Fall. When the leaders pointed to the Law of Moses as giving them the very permission to divorce that Jesus claimed God did not, Jesus put his finger on their duplicity. The reason for this law was not to give permission but to cause the man to pause from his mad pursuit of turning his wife out of his life unprotected. Knowing they were twisting this law to their advantage, Jesus openly proclaimed the reason for the law was that men's hearts were hard. In place of seeking to become the husband God wanted a man to be for his wife, he justified his failure as her fault. She must go. "Why, God, did you give me this woman?"

Some degree of hard heartedness is pretty universal among all who have unfinished business. Since we think we have said "Yes" to so much of what God has done for us through Jesus's death and resurrection, we may have been fooled into believing that a few "No's" can be part of the give and take of our relationship with Him. After all, we all have our limits. And we claim that we know them too. I once met with a group of leaders in a church who were caught in the throes of conflict between each other. After reminding them of the central characteristic that reveals to the world they are believers— loving one another—and walking them through the practices of mature believers of confessing, repenting, reconciling and restoring, the ringleaders decided that these truths did not count in this situation. They had a right to walk away from the congregation to whom they were responsible to be an example. Staying together and reconciling was too much to ask according to their way of thinking. Their limit had been reached and God could not expect more of them. Their collateral damage had spoken.

The hard heart is rationalized defiance plain and simple. For this reason, it is near to impossible for anyone to spot it in him or herself. It seems to make sense to disregard what Scripture says in a world so different from earlier times. It seems to make sense to make new applications of biblical mandates if they fit our cultural preferences. Even a cursory reading of the theological rationale for keeping people in slavery in America reveals rationalization so deep and so twisted from God's creating all men equal that today we are challenged on how Christians of that period adopted such thinking. The answer is simply they had hard hearts and even a bloody civil war did not persuade them otherwise.

And so people who are otherwise kind and thoughtful froth when confronted with the need to forgive those whom they hold in contempt. Or to surrender their rights. Or to submit to God's plan. Or to confess they were wrong. Or even to see that they were wrong. Their hard hearts will just not let them do so. They refuse to lose those confrontations.

Feelings. Fear. Hard Heart. These tell you something is wrong within your soul. Events you have seen through your damaged emotions have been wrongly interpreted. Statements you have heard others say to you in good faith you have twisted. The state of your soul tells you what you see, what you hear. And it is lying to you with your own voice. This is how damaged you are.

The worst part of all this is that where you are wounded is where you are love starved. Innately, people are seeking love in this world, whether they know this is their quest or not. You and everyone else were created for love. Wounds mark the dearth of love in that part of your soul. And the lie that damaged emotions play over and over again is that you are unlovable. So you have set off to find this missing love in all the places that are not God. This is the most devastating aspect of the damage, for we dismiss God as the source of all love, as the answer to our greatest need. And so your heart aches with pain from your wounds, and the Person who is the solution is not seen as a solution at all.

EMOTIONAL PRESSURE TO FIND RELIEF FROM THE PAIN

The *hurt of the heart* puts pressure on us to do something for the pain. We cannot live with pain. It is the same as if we physically hurt. If our headaches, we take aspirin. If it continues to hurt, we go to the doctor, if we can afford one. We could not get by in life if we let a broken arm go without a cast to immobilize it. Otherwise the physical pain would immobilize us.

As soon as our emotions start to hurt, we begin to look for a way to comfort our pain, consciously or unconsciously. I hurt, therefore I eat. Or drink. Or go sexually questing. I come home and turn on the TV to numb my mind from the pain of the day. I look for an escape. The deeper I hurt, the greater the internal pressure to find comfort. I look for ways to distract myself from the pain so that I will not have to think about it. Distractions do not heal the pain. The pain will be there when I get back from whatever activity I engage in. And so I will continue to look for the activity that will give me the longest period of relief and the best chance of quelling the pain, hoping in time it will lose its power to hurt me.

This pain opens us up to living out life in ways we would not necessarily choose rationally. What we are doing is running from the pain. This is the normal approach for all people. Since we cannot live with pain, and do not have it in ourselves to block the pain, we see the only path for us is to avoid it through making choices that will comfort that pain. For you to understand the results of these choices in you, you will have to explore what else the Heart Chart shows you about yourself.

If you desire to examine your history with God to discover your woundedness issues, please make use of the *Hurt of the Heart Inventory* found in Appendix 1. You may also download a copy which includes further information for processing these issues at: www.ChurchEquippers.com/ktdcresources/

4. CHOICES

YOUR ONLY CHOICES ARE ADDICTION OR HEALTH.

The workaholic who can afford all the goodies of life but his wife and children feel like he is a stranger. A depressed woman who spends her day wishing for a better life – or death. The person with five maxed-out credit cards. The guy who secretly watches pornographic materials on his computer. A person who is always thinking about and reaching for food. Someone who left her marriage for a married man. The father who beats his children when he is angry. A secret gambler deep in debt. A bitter person who is unable to look her family in the face. A man who floats from job to job, always complaining about the boss. The child who habitually lies to his parents and teachers.

What do all these people have in common? Two things. The first is that they are all wounded people. The second is that each has decided to comfort the wound he or she carries with equally destructive choices. More often than not, they chose this destination with their eyes open. This is true of everyone you meet, including the face in the mirror. The symptoms of what you chose to comfort your wound may not look like any of the ones mentioned in the previous paragraph, but they are just as damaging. This is an addiction choice. None of us are immune from the consequences of choosing comforting over healing.

We were not created by God to be able to handle pain in our souls. Because we cannot live with pain, we are looking for relief from the pain. That brings us all to the crossroads of choice. What we choose will take us towards gaining health or increasing the damage. While this is not a once-for-all-time choice, never to be revisited, regretted and revoked, choices are sending our lives towards one or the other destination every moment we live. It doesn't matter how spiritual you believe you are or how good an upbringing you had. Pain demands comfort and our background will not prevent us from choosing something for comfort which leads a destructive destination.

A friend of mine reached out to help a woman caught in a staggering situation. Raised by a secure family of Jesus followers, she married a promising young businessman. Together they experienced financial success and brought some great kids into the world. Then things went awry. The husband's improper business decisions led to a long prison term without parole. His assets were grabbed to pay back creditors. She was suddenly left with no money to live on and no job skills to market. All of these events—her husband's imprisonment coupled with the loss of their life together, plus the painful embarrassment of their situation and facing the future alone and untrained—were major wounds.

My friend hired her into his company and personally taught her all she needed to know to earn the kind of income she needed to live. Except, to the horrified astonishment of all who watched, she began to pursue a sexual relationship with a married man. My friend took her aside and counseled her time after time about the damage she was doing to herself and her children and how she was betraying Jesus. Nothing he said was heard. She mistressed the man until he finally divorced his wife. She divorced her jailed husband and they married. The rest of the story was full of sadness also.

Why did she do this? Nothing in her background even hinted she would live out a sordid story like this. She had never stepped outside the boundaries of decency, had been a loving daughter, wife, and mother. She never stopped going to church, even during her pursuit of this man. How did this happen? The answer is in how she *chose* to comfort her pain.

WHY PEOPLE MAKE DAMAGING CHOICES

Why does anyone make destructive choices when they could have chosen differently? If you want to understand the why of people's choices, look at the insights in Romans 6-7. Here Paul is dealing with the bogus notion that it doesn't matter how people choose to live life, because God will forgive everything in the end. In the middle of chapter six, he explains that those who believe in Jesus have been set free from the slavery of sin, which leads to death, and have become slaves of righteousness.

Then, in Romans 6:19, he points out to his readers that he is framing his response in human terms, because they are weak in their natural selves. This is a critical observation. His assertion that they are no longer slaves to sin does not mean they do not give in to sin anymore. They are human. They are weak. They can and do still choose to yield themselves to the powerful pull of sin. And they do know the effects that yielding to sin had on them before they were set free from the penalty of sin and received *zoe* life through Jesus. The point is plain. Paul is challenging them to choose to embrace this life instead of that which reeks of death, to yield themselves to righteousness instead of yielding to sin.

Paul unbends in chapter seven and tells them he himself struggles with yielding to sin. In this self-revealing passage, he shares that he does not understand his actions at all. He does things he does not want to do and he doesn't do the good things he desires to do. Even though he knows the right thing to do, he does bad things instead. In fact, God's holy commands produce a desire in him to rebel against them any way he can, and he can think of a few! His conclusion is, "As it is, it is no longer I myself who do it, but it is sin living in me" (Romans 7:17).

Pay attention to that statement. Although he has been freed from the penalty of sin, the power of sin still has deep roots in his soul. He'll end the chapter declaring what a 'wretched' man he is, meaning a miserable one—not an evil one. He is caught between his desire to be good for God and the reality of his life. I am sure you understand this kind of lament.

This passage brings me to the bottom area of the Heart Chart. What Paul is talking about in Romans is the *sin in me*, a cancer inside every one alive.

What is meant by *sin in me* exactly? Here is where I need to be clear or you will find yourself trying to address the wrong issues. The Romans passage is not speaking about particular actions or attitudes. For many people, this is hard to see. They have been brought up to think of sin as a list of forbidden actions. "Don't do this or that." If you keep the rules, you are a good person. If you break the rules, you're a bad person and God will punish you. This kind of formula for goodness and badness is pervasive in churches. People like this because it provides them a guideline to keep score by. They know they are good because they keep all the rules demanded of them.

What's more, they can spot the ones who are bad because those people are not living in line with the rules. Black and white. It's simple and easy to follow.

If you think this way, you are again failing to own how deeply you have been affected by the Fall. There can never be a list of rules that will cover all the choices you make, because doing what you prefer against God's reign over you is damaging even when you are living by rules that appear good. You will not get well by adding new rules to your list. This is not where the journey goes anyway. Paul makes that clear in Colossians 2:20-23. This church had been infiltrated by false teachers who were combining the truths of Jesus with the trappings of a legalistic morality, bleeding freedom out of their lives. Paul asks them, "Since you died with Christ to the basic principles of this world, why as though you still belong to it, do you submit to its rules: Do not handle! Do not taste! Do not touch!" Here is the first-century equivalent to religious performance that still misleads many people. Paul's conclusion puts a complete stop to the idea that rules are the answer to people's sin problem. "Such regulations indeed have an appearance of wisdom...but they lack any value in restraining sensual indulgence." That is the problem with rules. They have no power to fix what is really wrong with us, as spiritually wise as they might seem.

The journey you will need to pursue focuses on first understanding what this *sin in me* is that influences how you make choices, then on to why you make the choices you do. *Sin in me* is not about bad actions and being wicked. It is about becoming damaged by following the impulses of your desire to do what pleases yourself, by believing the lie that this choice will bring comfort to your pain apart from God. All sin harms you, tears the fabric of your soul, and leaves its hooks in you until you have given up your very life to it—unless you allow God to rescue you. That is the way you need to think about *sin in me*. It is the very root of all that destroys you and me. For that reason, we have to understand the nature of sin's influence.

SEVEN MOTIVATIONAL SINS WHICH ARE DEADLY

Many centuries ago believers defined the "what" behind their actions as the Seven Deadly Sins. For our purposes, we will call them motivational sins. They are deadly because they motivate people to pursue what kills their soul. All of them inhabit our hearts with potential, if not active, influence. Here is an overview of the seven:

Anger: Anger is more than just the powerful emotion of a wronged person. This motivational sin is a way of life for those in its clutches. It shows a strong desire for revenge – to get even – cultivating and harboring resentment. It argues, fights, or is sullen and silent. It is sarcastic, cynical, insulting, and critical. It counsels frequent irritation and desires harm for others, maybe leading to violence. We may regret the violence after anger has unleashed it—take for example people who have killed others in a moment of road rage—but at that moment violence seems so satisfying and right.

Let me clarify that here we are speaking of anger as a motivational way to live life, and not anger as the corrective tool God created as part of our emotional gear. Ephesians 4:26 notes the distinction between anger and sin. We can experience good anger. When we see someone bullying another person, or when a person intentionally offends us, God programmed us to feel anger so that we will seek to go about righting that wrong. This is natural and healthy anger. Anger shows itself to be a deadly sin when it festers inside and motivates us to want to hurt others instead of actively seeking restoration. This kind of anger is a way of life in which our desires and agendas guide its force. Anger as a deadly sin robs us of the sense of proportion in an offense, sees offence where there is none, and allows us to live with grudges even when those who have offended us have apologized. As it gets its hooks into us, we find we have no ability to let go of offenses, and they pile up in us as unpaid bills.

But the issue of anger as a deadly sin is rooted in the desire to have the power to compel compliance to our will. This is, in truth, a desire to be god over those who have offended us, to bring them to heel and make them fearfully bow to us. Much vengeful thinking motivated by anger involves dreaming about what we would do if we could work our will against those who have offended us. The motivational influence of anger is "I must control."

Lust: This is a sexual appetite beyond God's boundaries within marriage, an insatiable pursuit of sexual pleasure. Lust leads us to instrumentally use others, whether in pictures or in person, for our pleasure, rather than treating them as individuals of worth. 'Instrumental use' refers to using another person as if he or she were a tool, like a hammer or screwdriver, something possessing no feelings, made for a specific use. In other words, when you are motivated by lust you want a possession, not the person, to satisfy your desires. The reverse is also true. Lust will dull your self-worth until it drives you to want to be an object of desire in the eyes of others.

When lust becomes the influencer in you, you lose concern for another's well-being. No depth of relationship is built on lust, no matter how long the liaison lasts. Love that may have existed between two people is lost when they are in the grip of lust, because lust is ultimately about one's personal gratification and not about deep partnership built on intimacy. The motivational influence of lust is "I must have unlimited sexual pleasure."

Gluttony: The name of this deadly sin often misleads people about its influence on them. We tend to associate it with eating too much food, and with obesity. So if you are a disciplined eater and slim, you might reason that this deadly sin has no influence on you.

The ancient believers did not call it gluttony, however. Their title for it originally was "Appetite." It's about feeding any type of appetite with more and more of a certain thing. It can trigger an ever-increasing appetite for anything—drugs, chocolate, the Internet, spending, or work. It takes what is a natural interest or activity in us and intensifies the pull of it to where we do not feel satisfied with a natural amount of whatever it is. It creates a physical and emotional attachment of appetite to that interest or activity, so that we cannot just stop at normal.

Whatever you cannot get enough of is a signal that gluttony is at work in you. Becoming an alcoholic is the result of gluttony. But not all gluttonous activities appear so devastating. I knew a woman who had over 4,000 elephant figurines in her home. There was nowhere to move in her house *but she still wanted more.* Giving yourself over to any excessive activity represents gluttony. And the poison of gluttony is that it will direct you to spend all your fortune, time, and strength trying to satisfy the unquenchable appetite that has been unleashed in you. The motivational influence of gluttony is "I have to indulge."

Envy: Envy is the green-eyed monster that builds discontent with your lot in life. The focus is on other people in comparison to you. This motivational sin feeds your want for what someone else has, whether a material possession, position, popularity, or success. It is being in unrelenting competition with another, unhappy when someone else gets a break, secretly glad when that person suffers a setback. The emotion triggered by envy is discontent.

No amount of personal accomplishment on your part will quiet this motivational sin, because it focuses your eyes outward. Even when you have your own achievements to celebrate, you will always see them in light of other people's accomplishments. This comparison will diminish them in your eyes and allow you to continue life dissatisfied. The motivational influence of envy is "I deserve what they have."

Greed: This motivational sin is about what you worship, the true idol of your heart. It compels you to want more of what you adore than you already have – that you never really have enough. It doesn't have a specific item in focus; it just wants to accumulate more of everything. You find yourself stockpiling things instead of sharing, even with your family members. Greed could be an issue with you if you have an instant negative reaction when anyone asks for a bite of what you have on your plate. Greed causes you to feel overly distressed when you suffer even a minor loss.

In the most basic sense, greed plays on what constitutes security for you. For this reason, in many people greed is about money. Greed convinces you that if you can get and hold on to enough money, you will feel safe. But that you never really feel safe is the catch. One millionaire once replied to the question of how much was enough with, "Just a little more."

That is greed talk. In fact, greed intensifies your willingness to take dangerous risks to find this elusive security, so that reckless choices seem wise. The results can be disastrous. For example, one of the sad by-products in states that have legal gambling to raise revenues is the billboards advertising help for those who now have gambling addictions.

Even the acquiring of wealth does not mean you are now feeling secure. Greed can lead you to Ebenezer Scrooging your way through life, not enjoying what you have and unwilling to share with anyone else who is in need. Paul notes that some of the people under Timothy's oversight in Ephesus are "eager for money, have wandered away from the faith and pierced themselves with many griefs" (1 Timothy 6:10). In other words, greed will lead you from the real security of your faith in God to seek to find it in something else. The motivational influence of greed is "I want more and more."

Sloth: This is the most misunderstood deadly sin of the seven. That slothful people can be hard workers confuses others, since too many think of sloth as laziness. This motivational sin is not just about laziness, but an unwillingness to take responsibility for yourself. Sloth will lead you to not do what is necessary for your growth and health. "I can't change" and "It is not my fault" or "It's someone else's responsibility" are phrases used by people in the grip of sloth. Only doing the part of your work that you like and avoiding the rest is a sloth decision.

The Proverbs show us these two sides of sloth. Proverbs 6:6-11 warns readers that too much sleep (aka laziness) brings poverty to them. The other side is the slothful person who says, "There is a lion in the road, a fierce lion roaming the streets" (26:13). What this reveals is that the slothful person expects someone else to deal with the lion. It's not her responsibility.

You might be surprised what the emotional impact of sloth is on those caught in its sway. Some of the most common symptoms are sadness, feelings of helplessness, habitual procrastination, boredom, restlessness, and preoccupation with activities that have no value. Many people who make sloth choices end up suffering from ongoing depression. Anxiety and fear problems often have their root in sloth. Suicide can be an end product of sloth. The reason why is that sloth robs people of the feelings of self-worth and self-respect. As they lose the healthy sense of responsibility for their lives, hopelessness that life will never be better develops, especially since they lack the inner drive to own and influence their life's outcome.

You might see adult children who are constantly being rescued by their parents. They run out of money:. Mom and dad fork over. They end up in jail: Mom and dad bail them out. They lose their job, flunk out of school, wreck their marriage. No problem: Move back home with mom and dad. Mom makes my bed, cleans my room, and takes care of my kids. I won't go to work, watch television all day—fine. Mom and Dad cover for me. That's a slothful person. These people are especially in trouble when their parents die. They've got to find someone to do for them. A man might elect to allow others to do his work for him at the office and focus on becoming the all-time solitaire champion. For some, it might take the form of, "My home is a mess and I'm overweight and depressed but I just can't figure out why—it's too overwhelming to deal with." They don't want to be responsible for themselves. The motivational influence of sloth is, "I cannot so I don't."

Pride: This motivational sin is the underlying root of all sin. It is the root of the original rebellion against God's right to rule over us that goes way back to the Garden story. It is the one place in the Bible where God is said to be in open combat with a motivational sin. James 4:6 and 1 Peter 5:5 both quote Proverbs 3:34 where we are told, "God opposes the proud but gives grace to the humble."

Pride is ultimately about believing you are the center of your world. Secretly you believe you really ought to be God because you could run things so much better. It shows arrogance, an attitude of being superior to others. It is self-satisfied, anxious to get credit, desires to occupy the first place, is strongly opinionated, inflexible, and chafes under authority and the rule of God.

If you could step away from your pride, you might see the humor in all of humankind sharing the same belief. Perhaps we need a Hobbs for our Calvin, reminding us that the point of the creation of the world was not to bring us into existence! But for many, this is no laughing matter. People are seriously dominated by their own false view of their worth. So are you. So am I.

John Boys called it the last sin to die, for good reason.[4] Pride does so much to define our lives that we cannot possibly see how pervasive its power is over our thinking. It creates a protective perimeter, allowing us to think better of ourselves than we should and making it impossible for us to pursue becoming our real self. Even if we hate ourselves and label ourselves failures or some other nasty name, pride still guides us away from dealing healthily with the problems. One person noted you can find a twelve-step program addressing all the other deadly sins, but not for pride. The motivational influence of pride is, "I am the center so I will do it my way."

A personal inventory for you to examine how the deadly sins are affecting your life is available for you at: www.ChurchEquippers.com/ktdcresources/

THE FALSE COMFORT OF DEADLY SIN

Go back now to the *hurt of the heart*. The result of hurt is that your emotions are damaged. You do not want to feel pain. So what does the *sin in me* do? It offers you something to comfort your pain. It lies in suggesting, "Here is a way you can deal with what has happened in life so that you don't have to feel the pain." This is the functional deception of the *sin in me*.

And we are drawn to this deception that we can feel better without even addressing the *hurt of the heart*. We hurt already and do not want to add to our distress by facing this pain. So we choose to run from the pain and embrace the *sin in me*'s lie. Here is the answer. Let pain take care of itself while we ourselves are being actively distracted by the *sin in me*.

This is the hook of the *sin in me*. Why do we get caught in its web of lies? Because each deadly sin has an emotional component. Each sin offers you a feeling that blocks the source of your *hurt of the heart*. Instead of your pain, now you feel empowered by anger, you feel the sensuality of lust, and you experience the demandingness of sloth, or perhaps the numbing impact of feeding an appetite. These emotional narcotics pull you along and mask the fact that you are still hurt. Your comfort choice now has your psyche on emotional steroids. In the short run, we do feel better and we like it.

For example, take the guy who has been made to feel emasculated—that he is not a man—by one of his parents. (In fact, the internal struggle many men face involves manhood wounds.) What could he choose to comfort himself? Different options are open to him. Lust might lead him to sleep with lot of women to convince himself that he is a man. Or he might use anger to dominate others, letting him feel like a man. Or pride might propel him into competing and achieving in life to prove to his unseeing parent that he is really a man. If he has a weaker nature, he might indulge in the spite of envy towards someone who is more the man he wished he was. Or he might just give up and prove the characterization true by living a life of sloth. Or choose gluttony and go to the medicine cabinet, the liquor cabinet, the refrigerator, or the TV, or spend lots of money on toys—anything that will comfort him so that he will not feel the pain of not being thought of as a man. And he will go on to build a lifestyle around whatever he chooses. His preferred *sin in me* will mark him as long as he allows it to be his comfort for his *hurt of the heart.* This is not the same as dealing with the pain of emasculation.

Women, who are different from men in so many ways, fight different internal battles. There are two major wounding categories with which many women wrestle. The first is sexual abuse. Researchers suggest that one in four women have been abused by a close friend or family member during their childhood. The resulting damage is enormous. The second way women are wounded is related to self-image issues. This is not just about supermodels and airbrushed pictures. "How one looks matters!" is a message that's communicated to women early in their lives. In the smorgasbord of various comfort options, a woman might chose anger and become bitter towards those who snubbed their noses at her. Or she may select lust and seek to present herself as the object of desire to men, using sex to gain a sense of personal attractiveness. Or she may give herself over to gluttony choices and gain weight to fend off intimacy from men to save herself from expected rejection. Or she may succumb to envy and be unable to befriend other women whom she thinks have what she lacks. These comfort choices may be unconsciously made, but they tragically illustrate the typical means by which we end up where we don't want to be.

Harder to recognize are the layers of the *hurt of the heart* that open us up to believing the lie. We do not have just one pain for the *sin in me* to exploit. We have multiple wounds in our souls that we are choosing to comfort with deadly sin. The longer you live, the more *hurt of the heart* issues you are accumulating and the more *sin in me* choices you are making. This means lust or greed or anger may be comforting a multitude of unrelated hurts. This intertwining of hurt issues brings complexity to our healing process. This is what I mean when I say we do not know how deeply we have been affected by the Fall.

The impact of the *sin in me* is endless. What you choose depends on what draws you. These seven can be chosen singularly or in combinations to form a personal expression of their influence on you. Those who rape are choosing to act out on a blend of anger and lust to comfort their pain even as they pass out pain to their victims. People who squander away their paycheck are often operating out of a mixture of sloth and gluttony. Pride often dominates many of the combinations. While certain *sin in me* choices are more easily spotted, all of these deadly sins are in your heart and are influencing your life at some level.

Specific *sin in me* choices may be more attractive to you because they are found in your family of origin background. If you are drawn to greed, chances are that greed goes back generations in your family tree. If you are given to gluttony— say in the form of alcoholism—you may have been influenced towards this first at home. I once helped a man trace anger in his family tree. He was able to remember serious anger stories of his father, grandfather, and his great grandfather – three generations back. It gave him greater insight into his own choices.

Your *sin in me* choices are not limited to what may dominate your family of origin. Those choices could be influenced by personal bents in you that reflect the damaging impact of the Fall on your makeup. It could help you gain understanding why you have chosen to comfort yourself. But remember, no one has a right to a victim mentality. Your family is not responsible for your choices no matter how they live their lives. You can gather insight about their influence on you, but you must avoid blaming them for your choices. In the end you are the one—consciously or unconsciously—who chooses the *sin in me* that affects the health of your soul.

WHERE YOU GO FROM HERE

If you accept the truth of this (i.e. choosing sin in me to comfort the hurt of the heart), you might believe you now know enough to alter your choices. You might feel you have gained enough insight into your soul to make changes. If you think this, I counsel that you should expect to be disappointed because understanding about the *sin in me* is not enough. What you are struggling with goes deep. Since, not if, you have made choices about comforting your hurts, you must understand two other issues that come into play.

First, your *sin in me* choices have led you to addiction. What started out as comfort has taken firm root in your soul, so that you no longer are choosing *sin in me* but being controlled by it. The resulting symptoms of your choices have now become strongholds, held against even determined attempts by you, or those who love you, to overcome them.

Second, you lack the personal power to change at this level. To address something as controlling as the *sin in me*, you will need transformational power, not reformational power. I illustrate this to those I counsel this way:

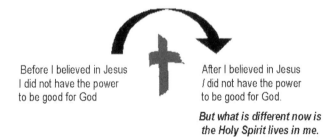

Before I believed in Jesus
I did not have the power
to be good for God

After I believed in Jesus
I did not have the power
to be good for God.

**But what is different now is
the Holy Spirit lives in me.**

Trying to change in your own power is an illusion. You may find yourself making lateral moves, using repression to tamp down the urges, trying hard to be obediently different, but not moving forward in the healing process. But the good news is that the power to be transformed is already present now in you. I will come back and tackle the issue of transformational power further after I explain some other important stuff.

5. ADDICTION

ALL SIN IS ADDICTIVE.

Once I participated in a leadership assessment for a group of young couples. After putting them through many interviews and observing them in a number of group interactions, the assessors gathered to shape their collective decision of each person's leadership readiness and abilities. One candidate's conduct in group dynamics stood out to me as inappropriate and intimidating, so I decided to mention this. I had intended to suggest that he needed mentoring in his personal leadership style but what came out of my mouth was a surprise even to me. I couched my views in personal terms, stating that I was *personally offended* by this person's actions and I had been treated like that by leaders like him!

What came to my mind almost immediately after I spoke was, "Where did that come from?" The vehemence behind those choice words was a way-over-the-top personal reaction to what should have been comments about the candidate's conduct. What I realized almost as soon as I spoke was that what I had said was a symptom of something wounded inside me that I had comforted by a *sin in me* choice. Because I had not chosen to allow God to heal me of wounds from previous leaders' mistakes, bitterness came out of my mouth. The bitterness was not the problem, but it was a signpost for all who were in that room that I was not whole.

This brings me to the next aspect of the Heart Chart. Your and my unfinished business is not invisible to an observer. When the *hurt of your heart* is comforted by the *sin in me* choice you made, it produces symptoms outside where almost anyone with a discerning eye can see it. And they do see.

When people come looking for help for their lives, the pain of their outward symptoms are the reason. Symptoms, such as anger or pornography or even success at the expense of one's family, are the collateral damage of unfinished business. People come to the place where either the symptoms are causing them distress and they want help or they have been directed by someone who has authority over them to deal with those symptoms. Because symptoms are the mostly visible part of unfinished business, people do think of them as the real problem. I say mostly visible because people are adept at hiding some of their most grievous ones. But all symptoms are ultimate results of the *sin in me* combining with the *hurt of the heart*. And some symptoms have been with people so long that they barely notice them at all. They feel natural and normal to them.

Given time, however, symptoms sprout their own brand of poison and begin to mess up all of our lives, adding to the wounds our hearts already bear. Relationships are damaged, marriages are lost, health is ruined, finances flow out to cover the costs of the symptoms. Symptoms can become so painful in themselves that we can get the impression it is the symptom that is destroying our lives instead of choices that nurtured it into life. And we become confused, disoriented. We no longer know what else hurts, what other unfinished business we have, because one or two symptoms are now dominating our life. Help is pushed away because we are angered by the hurt and embarrassed that people are noticing our symptoms out loud.

SYMPTOMS OBSERVED

Symptoms give us the opportunity to face the deepest truths about ourselves. The challenge for us is to not view the symptoms as primary truth about what is wrong, but as pointers to the truth about what is going on in us. When we can honestly take note of a symptom, we can be on our way to asking the question, "Where is this coming from?" We are being informed by the presence of the symptom that something in our soul is wounded and we have made the wrong choice on how to get well. Symptoms are an open door to turning toward God who will carry us down the path to wholeness.

This is a problem for us because we are self-protective, wanting the real issue to be something much more superficial and easily fixed, if it really needs fixing. After all, we reason, lots of stuff means nothing really. We are also comparers. We compare ourselves to other unfortunate symptom-bearers and seek to determine our personal healthiness based on those who are worse off than we are. One of the more tragic human behaviors is the practice of condemning others who have visible symptoms we disapprove of while nurturing symptoms ourselves that are equally damaging. "Well," we say, "at least I don't do (whatever)," as if the other person's whatever has drained our symptoms of their destructiveness. This somehow makes us feel better about ourselves for the moment at least.

A good step for you at this moment is to explore the symptoms you might have using the following inventory. The inventory potentially will allow you to gain personal insight about yourself. Take some time now and mull over the following categories of symptoms. They offer you some handles to what is damaging to your life.

- **Stuff you hide.** These symptoms are either embarrassing to you or would make you a social outcast if others knew. You choose to do these behind closed doors and hide them even from your family. You even plan times when you can do it so that no one will know.

- **Stuff you apologize for.** You have a way with words that come out of your mouth and choose actions regularly that tromp all over other people's feelings. We used to call these things "rude, crude and socially unacceptable." But you may have been practicing them so long that you have stopped apologizing and don't care what anyone thinks.

- **Stuff that irritates you in others.** Harsh judgment of others could be a primary indicator of what may be wrong with you. If how others live out their life, raise their children, think about politics, etc., pulls your chain, the irritant of their speck may be an unobserved log in your own eye (Matthew 7:3). People often attack stuff in other people with which they personally have problems but cannot admit it.

- **Stuff causing you pain.** You know you are going to hate yourself but here you go again. You knew you would be found out if you did it one more time, and you were right. You did these things with your eyes open and now the hurting has started again—physically, mentally, or emotionally.

- **Stuff that breaks relationships.** You have left a trail of broken friendships and lost companionships. People no longer call you and have blocked your text messages. And it is because of that thing you do and have defended as being okay for you to do. Except you are now lonely and feeling alienated from the ones that mattered to you at one time. If you honestly trace these broken relationships back to yourself (after all, you are what all these broken relationships have in common), you can discover symptomatic behaviors in you that were the beginning of the end of those friendships.

- **Stuff that wounds others.** From the people who have not left your life or even people who you come into casual contact with—for example a waiter, customer service rep, neighbor up the street—you are getting an 'ouch' reaction. Some of them roll their eyes when they see you coming. You have not yet heard their pet names for you, but the names are not pretty. What are you doing or saying that is causing the ouch?

- **Stuff that increasingly costs you more and more resources.** What you used to love in moderation now is robbing you like a thief. More and more of your time and money is becoming wrapped up in maintaining your pet behaviors.

- **Stuff that you cannot stop doing.** You promised yourself "This will be the last time" the last time you did it, but here you are at it again. These symptoms are set off by the obsessive/compulsive button in you. There is an excessive attachment within you that connects you with these symptoms. Many of these started out as good things to do or be but now are lived out like an extreme sport. You find you cannot live without them.

- **Stuff that you cannot see in yourself.** This may seem like an impossible category to assess, but actually it is quite simple. All you have to do is remember the comments you have received from loving friends, family, and well-wishers who have risked offending you by mentioning some damaging behavior or attitude in you. You can't see it. But they told you for your own good(!) sometime in your past. What symptoms did they quiz, warn, or tell you about? Or by what nickname are you known, to your chagrin?

Why bother with this inventory—in case you are tempted to skip it? The truth is that what is a symptom in your life today may become an addictive behavior or attitude—might already have even—that will dominate your life. All symptoms are equal in their capacity to damage if not yet equal in their destructive power over each person's life. Some of you may be at the front end of the appearance of a new symptom. Others of you may be dog years into living under a symptom's tyrannical reign. So even if you have a great cover story for your symptom—"It's a family trait," or "I'm just stressing right now"—in time the symptom you have will become the master and you the slave.

WHY WE DO NOT NATURALLY ABANDON OUR BAD CHOICES

So why don't we just chuck the symptoms when they

become a problem? Let's talk some more about the deadly sin that is in our heart. The main issue we have to face is that comforting ourselves by sin is a personal choice. It may be consciously or unconsciously made, but it is our decision. The person who wounded us did not force us on that path. No outside being put a gun to our head to make us go in this direction. The devil didn't make us do it. Deciding to comfort our wounds by sin is not even an age or maturity issue. At its root, it involves three forces at work influencing us that we may not even perceive at the time.

The first is our depth, or lack of depth, of intimacy with God. All of us know that God has the right to reign over our lives. Doctrinally, we can recite the right beliefs and quote the right passages. But the flaw revealed in us through the Fall is our desire to blame God for our mess. This desire often gets in the way of our intimacy with Him. We withdraw even while we are busy serving Him and the church, and then feel empty and wonder why He demands—or why His people demand—so much of us. Then new wounds come up or old ones come out. We become angry at Him for not appreciating our obedience, our sacrifice, and yet we deny that anger. After all, how can we hold God accountable? So we reroute the anger and find ourselves in a place where the *sin in me* feels a whole lot better than listening for His voice. It is hard to ask God to heal us when we, at some level, are blaming Him as Adam did.

The second is the role modeling that has taken place in our

personal world. When the people of our world, who can also be the source of our wounds, model certain kinds of sinful choices in their own lives, we secretly resonate with them, even when rationally we are repelled. For example, people who have had a bad home life grow up saying they will never be like their parents. Except they often find they really are just like their parents—when they have children. The DNA for that metamorphosis was implanted through the role modeling they endured. Sin begets sin. We know this action was wrong when so and so did it, but it makes so much more sense to us now we are choosing the action.

The third is how open we are to the lies of Satan. When we find ourselves out of intimacy with God, the truths we hold have a way of becoming twisted and sounding hollow. Satan shows up with his pretty lies. He speaks to our bruised egos. He sympathizes over our wounds. He suggests a way of hopeful recovery. Satan lies to us every day, until his lies begin to take on the veneer of reality and we try his suggestion "just this once."

Except it never is just this once. *All sin is addictive.* READ THAT AGAIN! Do you understand what this means? It means that in a very short time the sin you choose will take charge of your will and you will no longer be able to choose not to do it. Your damaged emotions will press you to do it again and again until you give in. You will feel emotional pressure or release based on your response to the power of the addiction. You will not be able to stop yourself. And in time you will rationalize it. In case you missed it, a disgraced former political leader asked his wife for permission to go see his mistress after he confessed his affair! That kind of addiction will happen to anyone who buys into Satan's lies. It is the last stop in the matter of choice.

What is more, the addictive behavior has now become a source for further wounding. This is the irony of choosing sin for comfort. I was wounded and chose to comfort myself with one of the deadly sins in my heart. Now I am wounding myself as the result of that choice and am in a worse place than before. "Hmmm... what sin will I choose to comfort me now?"

SYMPTOMS BECOME ADDICTIONS

When you finally get down and dirty about your symptoms, you may come to the point of admitting they are really addictions in development. Some have already crossed that line and own you. Others are still vying for that level of control and, left unattended, will eventually get power over you. Do you know how symptoms progress to addiction? If a symptom is the product of comforting the pain of your woundedness, the fact that your wound is not getting better is the key. It hurts and the way you are comforting it will not make it hurt less. After a while you begin to develop a tolerance for the comfort activity. Tolerance means that you have become used to it in a way that it no longer covers the pain as it did. You need a stronger dose of whatever it is to calm the throbbing.

This dwindling power of tolerance leads you to a crossroads. When—and if—you try to stop dosing your wound with this comfort activity, you will suffer withdrawal, either physically or emotionally or both. You could quit at this moment if you did not still hurt. But where you end up is becoming restless and being irritated at those around you. Withdrawal symptoms then become an emotional force to push you back towards continuing the same activity. The other way at the crossroads leads you towards behavior in which the activity becomes central to your life. You may think about it obsessively until it merges with your personality and becomes an outward expression of who you now are. And you will find you no longer control it—it controls you. In the words of one person who has been there, "What grabs a toehold in your life progresses to a stronghold, then it gains a stranglehold over you." The word people use for this phase is 'compulsive.' You say you don't have to but you just cannot stop.

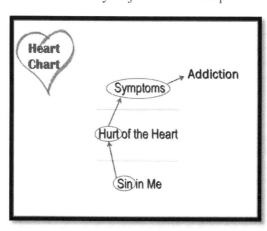

There is nothing inside you that can stop addictions' march to mastery. And once they have power over you, you can no more easily shed them than you can shed your skin. You can no longer free yourself. The *sin in me* is not about comforting your pain, it is about controlling you. The lie of the enemy always leads to death. Addiction is part of the journey to death.

You may be confused by the use of the word addiction. All of your life you may have associated it with drug users or alcoholics. Certainly they are addicts. That you are fortunate not to have such addictions does not mean you have nothing as powerful unhealthily driving your life. In fact, like everyone else you are impelled by forces you do not even notice because their addictive nature is as much a part of your life's fabric as breathing. You are much more adept at noticing other people's addictions than your own.

In a perverse way, addiction makes idolaters of us. In spite of its hellish nature, its power has drawn us into worship of our symptoms, to elevate their importance to us above God and what He wants for us. This obstinate devotion to our symptoms prevents us from truly and freely loving God and other people. We are trapped into venerating what we will come to hate. In time we will find our new god is a terrible one, demanding and destroying. This god is the absolute enemy of your freedom and the killer of love. All addictions lead to aloneness, which is hell. Carried on by the non-believer, it is their ultimate destiny—to be alone forever without receiving or giving love because their choices have led them there. But for the believer, to be in hellish aloneness is to live in the lie of the enemy.

Addiction upends one of our cherished beliefs—that we live our life with a completely free will through which we have the freedom to choose or not choose to participate in whatever we want. Free will is only partly true. We may choose what we want at the start, but as we go along, we find we cannot not do it. Addiction means we have become attached to something in an unhealthy way. Attachment comes from a French word meaning 'nailed to.' Our will gets nailed to a behavior or attitude and it becomes a way of life for us. In other words, what we freely choose at the beginning becomes compulsory. And not only becomes compulsory; it also demands payment. This is the robbery aspect of addiction. If left unchecked, it will take all you have—yourself—and leave behind a husk of a person whom your mother will love but not recognize.

This is not only true for those things we might consider to be bad, such as striking people when we are mad or smoking or cheating at games of skill. We find that normal life activities become distorted by our use of them for comfort. We become addicted to food, sex, leisure, education, relationships, work— anything that is touched by our *sin in me* choices. Why do people become addicted to prescription medicine, which was meant to help them get well? Why can't some people pass up a dessert or two or three even after their weight has ballooned to obesity? Why has Internet pornography become such a problem? This is just a sampling of uncomfortable questions. The scope of addiction is so broad that a complete listing of potentially addictive activities is impossible.

What you will become attached to will depend on your personal bent. Not everyone is affected the same way by the various *sin in me* choices. For example, lust affects people in different ways. In some it produces a desire for pornography with masturbation, or serial sex with multiple partners. For others it may become a pursuit of the illusive ultimate sex within marriage, leading him to use his wife for sex two or three times a day, but never achieving satisfaction, certainly not intimacy. Or one's bent might run in for collecting shoes as fetishes, or to incest, or to homosexual acts with little boys. Another might expose herself in a public place. Or consume steamy romance novels by the truckload. These are just a taste of the addictions that result from lust. Which one grabs you depends on the makeup of your psyche. The bent of one person might repel another, but not make him or her immune to addiction to a different expression of lust.

But for each person, addiction is seeking to fill a bottomless emotional neediness. Addiction is not about what the person is addicted to, it is the inability to suck out of that object or activity the love he or she is seeking for becoming whole. That is also why religious activity can also be addictive. Jeff VanVonderan says of this spiritual addiction: "Working addictively for God is still working addictively."[5]

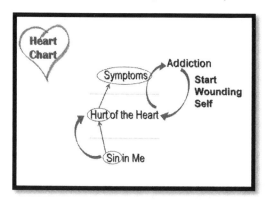

What happens next is the pattern of all addictions. At some point, your addiction begins to wound and rob you. The addiction that has taken over your life and directed your mouth and actions leads you to a place where you start losing things that you don't want to lose—home, spouse, job, health, children, wealth and more. You lose your way. You watch your best friends avoid you as more relationships are broken. Your body or your mind breaks down. If you continue in your addiction long enough, you can go into a death spiral, finding yourself in a place you never wanted to go. You essentially come to the pit and are willing to jump in with your eyes open.

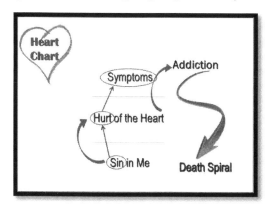

There are two truths you have to acknowledge about addiction if you are going to find freedom. The first is that addiction is powerful; much more powerful than you. This is not just about drugs or alcohol. All addictions are powerful. You will not be able to stop on your own, no matter how hard you try. Whatever you are addicted to has allied itself with your damaged emotions. Through them, it is ruling over your will even when your rational thoughts warn you of its destructive work. Your mind can see where the addiction is leading you, but your so-called free will will not respond with a rescue, even if you are on the brink of death. That's how powerful addiction is.

Perhaps you think your addiction is the exception. This is rationalization at work. We tell ourselves this act or attitude won't really hurt us. That is because we have the short view of what is happening. The long view is that all addictions lead to the pit. Period. With time, yours will too. If you will not accept this truth, you will not turn to God for your rescue.

The second truth is that you really enjoy what you are addicted to. They are pleasure activities. It's no use Christianizing our dilemma. We look at pornography because we like to see naked people. We get even with those who hurt us and love it. We revel in overeating—you cannot have too much pie! Our road rage is justified, and do we ever feel righteous. There is always tomorrow to find a job, so we enjoy our TV marathon today with no guilt. And who doesn't love spending money, even if we will have to rob Peter to pay Paul? Whatever our addiction, we do it again and again because it makes us feel good at some level, even though it is leading us to destruction. We lie to others, even ourselves, on this point because we know we are supposed to hate sin. But it is such fun! It is this aspect of addiction that draws us in even as we desperately ask Jesus to rescue us. Admitting you like doing what you do is honest and opens the door for a real relationship with God.

NEEDING JESUS TO DELIVER AND HEAL

Now we know why people like us who are caught in the tangle of the *sin in me* do not listen to wise spiritual counsel. The emotional blare of our sin addiction is louder than the truth of God—and the love of God. But no one's tale has to end in despair and destruction. We can choose even now to surrender to Jesus, who alone is able to overcome addiction in us through two powerful actions. The first is for Him as the king who reigns over us to deliver us from the *sin in me*. This is obvious. That is why God sent Jesus into the world in the first place. Sin produces brokenness in us, breaking not only our relationship with Him, but causing the damage that only He can repair.

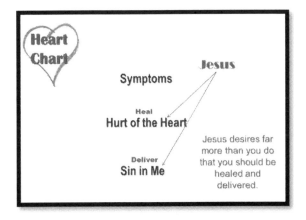

While we may want Jesus to deliver us from our symptoms, our real need is not for a particular addiction to come under His rule, but the *root cause* of that addiction. Not just gambling—but greed. Not just pornography—but lust. Not just selfishness—but pride. We need Jesus to reign completely over our deadly sins because we do not yet recognize all the symptoms we are battling anyway.

Yielding to Jesus' reign over the *sin in me* is not enough, however. To break from the power of sin, we also need Jesus as the Great Physician to heal the *hurt of the heart*. Healing is the necessity for our souls. If we do not allow Jesus to touch the hurt, closing ourselves off to His examination and prescription, then we are doomed to repeat the cycle of hurt, comfort and addiction for as long as we resist. You see, we cannot live with hurt. We naturally look for ways to stop the pain. If we say to Jesus that He can reign over the particular motivational sin that for years we have used to soothe the *hurt of the heart*, another of the remaining six will offer comfort in its place. A new addiction will appear out of this choice, different from the first one, but in time just as damaging.

This is the point where many people stop. As mentioned before, our wounds really do hurt. We would rather God not go there and touch them because of how badly they hurt. Let me encourage you not to choose to stop but to go on. Courageously risk something with Jesus instead of putting off healing. If you do not, addiction will rule your life again in time.

If this is making some sense to you, you may think you are ready to become whole again. If so, there is a question you have to face...

6. DO YOU WANT TO GET WELL?

YOU HAVE TO ANSWER THIS QUESTION.

While counseling Lorna, who was separated from her husband, I noticed that our conversation paralleled one we had many months before. The same accusations, the same anger, the same tears. She was stuck in the saddest possible way. I have watched people slipping into dark places with their eyes open, nailing their flag to the proposition that their being stuck is someone else's fault. Or they have tried everything to get unstuck—to act better, to be more spiritual, to forgive—all without success. I recall a woman named Ruth recounting all the spiritual exercises she had practiced in the hope of being granted freedom by God, but still found herself captured by her inner disquiet and bitterness because God was not holding up His end. The bitterness was affecting all areas of her life.

LIVING WITH A STUCK IDENTITY

In John 5, Jesus spies a man by the pool of Bethesda who was thirty-eight years stuck because he had no one to help him into the pool to be healed. The rumor about this pool was that an angel came and stirred it every now and then. People believed that the first one in after the stirring would be made well. Jesus' question to him was, "Do you want to get well?" In other words, "Is wellness really your goal and desire or, after thirty-eight years, are you so attached to your identity of the old guy at the pool who's been here since the days of Herod the Great that you are settled on finishing out the rest of your life being sick?"

All people have some form of stuck identity. A number of them wear it proudly. "That's just the way I am. Deal with it" they say. Their aggressive in-your-face ownership of this identity makes you feel you are in the wrong to notice. Others hate to have their stuck identity mentioned. They become angry or withdrawn when the subject comes up—their defense against having to deal with it. Everyone else knows about it, but is either too polite to say anything or too tired of the volcano unleashed every time he or she has tried to help the person who is stuck. No change is expected and none takes place.

So Chuck stays Mr. Angry. Let no one push his buttons. Amanda morphs into a power-play ranger at work. Jenny persists in her thoughtlessness. Bob maintains his back-stabbing ways. Carmen remains always depressed. Stuck identities are limitless—alcoholic, liar, two-faced, rude, insensitive, panicky, gossip, loud-mouth, negative, unkind, druggy, lecherous ,withdrawn, shopaholic, shallow, sarcastic, controller—too many to mention. Stop and ask yourself: With what identity am I known by the people who know me? Is this how I want to be remembered? Does this reflect the character of Jesus in me? Am I settling to live out life as something less than my created self?

And what is this identity? It is a product of the symptoms of your unfinished business. The stuck identity, regardless of how long it has been a part of you or how dominating it is over your life, is merely the evidence of a *hurt of the heart* issue that has been soothed by a *sin in me* choice. The resulting combination has become so ingrained in you that it has become a way of life, a noticeable characteristic as prominent as a wart on someone's nose.

We have to answer Jesus' question up or down, yes or no. There is no middle ground—no maybe. Our answer opens or closes the door to a healing process by which we shed this identity to which we have become stuck. We are invited by the question to take another step in conforming to the image of Jesus. I mean, can you imagine Jesus being whiny? Or ogling women? Or being judgmental towards the hurting people around him? Or ruining someone's reputation through gossip? Not hardly. When Jesus appears with this question on his lips, we are looking at the person whose identity God purposed for us to mirror.

Moreover, it is Jesus' death and resurrection that revealed our true identity—our created self. He became sin for us so that we could become the righteousness of God (2 Corinthians 5:21). To be righteous means to be totally perfect, without sin or guilt. To be fully in tune and reconnected with God. That is our identity. Not this broken, less than stellar, settled-for identity that is always the product of damaging choices. Even if we learn to live with this identity or worse, come to love what we have become, we are still stuck at being less than what we truly are. Does this bother you? If so, how will you answer the question?

RISKING IT ALL WITH JESUS

The Bethesda pool man's response is interesting. Winnowed down to its essence, he said that he had never been first. He had tried over and over again to get well, to get into the pool when the angel stirred it, but failed. On top of it, no one ever tried to help him be first. It's just the reality he lived with year in and year out as long as he could remember.

His response is the refrain we all sing at some time when confronted with this most significant question that Jesus asks. Do you want to get well? Well, do you? "Yes, but..." And we fill in the rest of that sentence with our conviction that no one cares to help us and all our failed solutions—personal retreats, continual confession, spiritual disciplines, repression of desires, accountability to others, self-denial, devouring relevant books, counseling sessions, weeping and crying before the Lord. What's wrong? We were so sure that this time we would get it right. What is so different in this hinted-at offer in Jesus' question that we have not tried already and received nothing for our pain? Especially since we now know we are further down the spiritual road towards inward despair and outward disaster. Do I want to get well? What kind of question is that?

It is a question of risk. For the man at the pool, it was about leaving the security of a way of life, of people feeding, clothing, and carrying him daily to his appointed place by the pool. But the risk was more than that. Jesus invited him to risk all to take up his mat and go home—on a Sabbath day. On the day when work was forbidden and carrying a mat in a public place courted stoning by the mob. It was about trusting that Jesus really knew what the man needed to do. And instead of negotiating, he just did it.

Are you willing to risk that you may be wrong about your preferred approach to spiritual health, that it may be part of your problem? That instead of being ruthless, you are choosing a risk-free bridge to nowhere? And as a result, your anger at God has grown? Perhaps you feel hopeless. Certainly you are stuck. What would it take for you to come to the place where you could really experience the healing grace of God?

Let me present two ideas for you to consider. First, you will have to risk letting God deal with the pain you and time have buried. At first glance this may not appear to be good news. After all, what no one wants is to feel the throbbing edge of that pain again. Yet God does not want to make you face the *hurt of the heart* as much as He intends to take you through it until you are healed. This is a risk moment, when you take up your bed and walk. The longer you hold out on this point, the longer you lay by the pool sick.

Second, if you choose to ask Jesus to deliver you from the

sin in me and heal you from the *hurt of the heart*, then you must start by coming to the end of yourself. You have messed up. You, not the people who hurt you, but you personally have made the choices that have bound up your life spiritually. You must own your sinful choices to comfort your pain. You must admit to the Father you have no wisdom deep enough, no spiritual strategies sweeping enough, no personal resources thorough enough to free you from the lies of the enemy. The first Beatitude is your benchmark. You indeed are poor in spirit because you have nothing in your arsenal that works. Your best strategies and deepest thoughts have not led you to the life Jesus is giving you. You are stuck because you have believed otherwise. To give up any pretense of knowing how to fix yourself, even by using the ploys that you have dressed up with religious jargon—this is freedom, not failure. To say to God, "I have failed in all I tried," is the kind of humility to which God responds, "God opposes the proud, but gives grace to the humble" (James 4:6; 1 Peter 5:5). It's the stuff that spiritual rest is made of for the believer.

Here is one more critical thing you have to know to get well. You chose your way. You did not deserve the wounds that have caused the hurt in you. But you chose how you would deal with the pain without asking Jesus. Until you own that choice, you can never say "Yes" to the question. Notice I said, "can never" and not, "will never." I know lots of people who verbally said "Yes" to Jesus' question. But because they only wanted him to take away their pain, maybe bring judgment on the person who wounded them, they ultimately found they lacked the ability to risk it all with Jesus to get well.

Think about the end of the man at the pool's story. After the healing, Jesus finds him in the temple, probably giving a thanks-for-the-healing sacrifice required by the Law, and tells him, "Stop sinning! Or something worse will happen to you." Strong words. Jesus is saying that just because you thought you were doing all you could to be healed does not mean you addressed the real issues in your life. So it is for all of us. We may minimize our choice of the *sin in me* to comfort our hurts and even rationalize our choices. Or celebrate freedom in one area so as to ignore the real lies we have hooked our wagon to. Stop lying to yourself that you haven't made a *sin in me* choice. For the life that we have been given in Jesus is far more fulfilling than any identity we have built by comforting our pain with the *sin in me*.

KNOWING YOURSELF

Maybe you are ready to stop lying to yourself. Where do you start the healing process? If you say "Yes" to the question, what's next? Next you must gain true insight about yourself. It starts with seeking to find out from God where all this pain came from. What is really going on inside your heart? What you are looking for is not self-knowledge, but transformational knowing.

The best way to understand the idea of transformational knowing is through the encounter between Jesus and Peter in Luke 5. Peter and his crew had been fishing all night without catching so much as an old boot. He then allows Jesus to use his boat as a speaker's platform to address a large crowd that had gathered on the beach to hear Jesus teach. Afterwards, Jesus suggested that Peter take his boat out deeper and throw out his nets again. Mildly protesting, Peter does and is surprised by the catch of a lifetime.

Something shifts in Peter's soul at this moment. His understanding of who he was dealing with deepens and, as it does, he sees his soul naked before Jesus. This was not just another man who had a knack for speaking, a religious teacher who wowed people with his insights. Peter perceives that Jesus is someone who possesses such connection with God that he knows things beyond the ordinary, including the hidden Peter.

He goes to his knees before Jesus and says, "Go away! Lord, I am a sinful man." Here is a successful businessman suddenly finding he cannot hide behind his stuck identity. Why? Not because of anything Jesus says, but because of who Jesus is. The contrast between Peter's identity and what he perceptively sees in Jesus makes it plain to him that he is stuck in spite of his fishing business success. This encounter overwhelms him.

Jesus makes clear that he will give Peter a new identity—an effectual identity of being a fisher for men—completing who Peter really is—a fisherman. If you know the rest of the story, you know this came to pass. This is his true created self. Peter did not become someone else. Peter did not abandon who he was so much as there was a stripping away of all that was damaging who he really was.

Peter's changed perception of Jesus and himself is transformational knowing. Peter had met Jesus before this spur-of-the-moment fishing trip. But this time he saw his own life in light of Jesus and didn't like what he saw. He knew in that instant that he had unfinished business. Up till then, Peter was either comfortable or at least had come to terms with who he was—until he met with Jesus in this way. The encounter opened his eyes to see the difference between what he could be and what he really was. Until that point, Peter could be said to have been unconnected from his created self. This is why stuck identity is a danger to you and me. It lulls us into believing we genuinely know ourselves. We falsely reason that if we must change, it will always be up to us to bring it off. But what if you don't know yourself as well as you need to? What if you discover you are living comfortably with the damaged you? And what if you truly lack the power to change? What then?

You may not be comfortable with these questions. Facing them panics most people, for a number of reasons. For example, you may be reacting badly because you think God is disgusted with you as a person and now you will have to admit He is right to feel that way. Or you may be operating under the delusion that your private efforts are already moving you towards your goals of bringing about personal change. So you want to close your ears lest these questions shake that dream. Or you might be the person who is worried deep down that you will never measure up, especially if you are going by the criticisms you grew up with coupled with too many of the sermons you took in on Sundays. I can remember multiple meetings with one man who had been beaten up by strong personalities most of his life, all of whose agenda was to preach to him about his need to change. My invitation to enter into a transformational process with God sounded to him like more of the same through his life-experience filter. And so he continued to dodge the question and stayed stuck.

Transformational knowing ultimately is about facing the deepest truths about ourselves. What you will discover in the process is that the symptoms produced by making *sin in me* choices to comfort the *hurt of the heart* wounds are not the primary truth about who you are. The good news behind transformational knowing is what a loving God intends for you and me—restoration to the whole person we were created in him to be. However, what the presence of our symptoms tells us is that we have settled for living with self-deception. This is a defense mechanism that our psyche automatically kicks in to falsely save us from facing unpleasant truths about ourselves. Seeing ourselves through transformational knowing retriggers the pain our self-deception has been trying to hide. This does not come easily. In fact, confronting self-deception is as difficult as flying an airplane through a one foot gap between two skyscrapers. In *The Gift of Being Yourself*, David Benner notes, "The penetration of our delusions is enormously challenging. It requires a relentless commitment to the truth and a deep sense of freedom from fear of rejection."[6]

If you are honestly looking for God to bring about deep change in you, the starting point is to openly ask Him to do a ruthless search in your life that will bring about this transformational knowing. Asking for a ruthless search is saying to God that you are ready to hear truth about yourself, to open up yourself to having closed areas of your soul—on which you have hung a "Keep Out!" sign—penetrated. "Closed," as in not wanting to revisit the pain because you did not know what to do about it. Closed, because you thought time would heal or had healed the wounds. Closed, because you decided it was a waste of time. Closed, because you wanted so badly to forget and get on with your life.

If you want to know how to enter into this search with God, consider the promise of the first affirmation. God is in the process of conforming you to the image of His Son, Jesus (Romans 8:29). Here is the entry point for joining God in the search: Where is your life not conforming to the image of Jesus? How do your life actions and attitudes line up with Jesus? This should not lead to an 'Of-course-I'm-not-perfect-like-Jesus' moment. This is for a ruthlessly honest "Ah-Ha! I see that this area of my life is out of line with who I am created to be," realization. You will know when you have gained real insight from God's search because ruthless honesty also sparks humiliation and true guilt—a "Woe is me!" response similar to Isaiah's in the temple when he saw the Lord (Isaiah 6:5). Your absolute helplessness and need for God will be magnified like never before.

There is hope. God offers a true healing, no matter how addicted one is to a stuck identity. But it is a hard path for us to embrace. It takes us *through* the pain of our wounds, not away from it. Yet never alone—you always have God glued to your side.

Furthermore, God has already endowed you with the power you need for restoration. Peter stated this boldly in his second letter, "His divine power has given us everything we need for a godly life through our knowledge of Him who called us by his own glory and goodness. Through these he has given us his very great and precious promises, so that through them you may participate in the divine nature, having escaped the corruption in the world caused by evil desires" (2 Peter 1:3-4). Peter is proclaiming that God is making sure you have all the power from Him that you need to be restored to your created self. And this power to transform is not something for which you are waiting to arrive like some long-lost UPS package. You have divine power available to you since the day you crossed the line of faith. It flows through your soul in a continuous stream of living water. You may be ignorant of this power, unpracticed in accessing it, but that doesn't lessen the reality of its presence within you.

RECEIVING MERCY AND OBTAINING GRACE

The biblical word for this power is "grace." Grace provides the counterpoint to mercy. Critical for our journey is how we understand and utilize these two actions of God. Many people have some confusion over what each means. I find that even well-known Bible teachers I respect have difficulty making the distinction clear between mercy and grace. Because we use these words almost synonymously, one can get the impression mercy and grace are the same. "Have some grace on that person," we say when we mean mercy. Yet in Hebrews 4:16 the writer clearly sees the two as distinct gifts from God. We "receive mercy and obtain grace" for our time of need. *This difference is our lifeline to the life Jesus promised.*

The writer of Hebrews challenges us to come into God's presence with confidence. This may seem beyond you as you grapple with the question about getting well. Maybe you feel you cannot talk to God about anything significant in your life. One reason might be because you have a strong sense of shame and guilt. You have not performed well in your life and are certainly aware of how badly you have done. You have let Him down. And so you feel you cannot face Him. Or perhaps you belong to the tribe who believe you are capable of getting your act together and you are supposed to handle your own healing process. Your faith community is deeply enmeshed in the "obedience" model. Or maybe you are just confused because you have never heard of this before.

Regardless of which it is, God doesn't need you to clean up or to take charge. But He does need you to understand His purpose. God wants you to be in his presence so that you can receive two things that you desperately must have from Him. Two things which you cannot get anywhere else. These are the mercy and grace about which the writer is speaking, both of which are totally undeserved, but you get them from God anyway.

Mercy happens when God withholds judgment that we deserve. And do we ever deserve judgment—every day—often—without end. But for those who belong to Jesus, there is now no condemnation (Romans 8:1). This is where God meets us in our wretchedness and makes it possible for us to come back. We prodigals would never be able to return to our Father if He did not open His arms to us.

Mercy is a covenant word. Covenant is a strange concept for people today, but essentially it is about people choosing to pledge themselves into a deep relationship breakable only by death. This pledge has been sealed by a blood sacrifice to illustrate the death pact. Note that the emphasis is on relationship by choice, not obligation. The word that defines God's covenant is *agape*, which is a willful love based on what the lover chooses, not on the choice of the loved one. There was nothing to compel God, who has no equal, into a relationship with humans who had decided they had no need of Him. Yet He deliberately delighted in doing it (Ephesians 1:5). The covenant God established through the cross portrayed an infinite being pursuing an unbreakable relationship with people like you and me.

When you and I ask for mercy, we are appealing to this covenant. Mercy characterizes our relationship to a superior who continues to love us when we mess up. Mercy is His love in action, much like a mother loving an exasperating child. Judgment is suspended, even if the consequence of our choices pains us still. You and I need mercy everyday due to our historical—and current—appalling choice to listen to the lies of the enemy. In His presence, we receive it.

Grace is significantly different from mercy. Grace is so much more than the forgiveness mercy delivers, because we need so much more. It is God's participation in our lives so we can be what we were made to be. You have to understand that grace is a power word. God is not only in the business of withholding judgment from us. God actually is enabling us to do what He wants us to do. Grace is God's empowering presence in us in the person of the Holy Spirit to transform us from what we were, changing us step by step into the image of Jesus.

Possibly you have never heard grace talked about as

power. Is this what grace is? Is it in the Bible or am I just engaging in wishful thinking? A number of passages present grace in just this way. One is where Paul talks about his thorn-in-the-flesh problem with the Corinth church. You know the story. Paul is explaining that his thorny messenger was from Satan to keep him from conceit over how much God had revealed to him. He prayed that God would take it away but God's response was, "'My grace is sufficient for you, for my power is made perfect in weakness.' Therefore (Paul continues) I will all the more gladly boast of my weaknesses so that the power of Christ may rest on me" (2 Corinthians 12:9). Here God is connecting his grace in Paul's life to the working of His power in and through Paul's life. God is using the thorn's presence to conform Paul's life by His grace. No matter how weak I am in myself, Paul reasons, God's power (read "grace") rests on me.

And then there is what Paul wrote in Ephesians concerning Jesus' resurrection in 1:19-20: "That power is like the working of His might strength which he exerted in Christ when *He raised him from the dead and seated him at His right hand in the heavenly realms.*" In this passage, Paul employed the entire first century thesaurus of the words related to "power" to describe how God accomplished this one-of-a-kind historical act. Yet in a stunning parallel, Paul describes our own salvation in similar terms in the next chapter: "But because of His great love for us, God, who is rich in mercy, made us alive in Christ even when we were dead in transgressions—it is by grace you are saved. *And God raised us up with Christ and seated us with him in the heavenly realms in Christ Jesus*" (Ephesians 2:4-7). Where Paul had used his entire vocabulary on power in the first chapter, he summed up God's work in one word here—grace. Love and mercy denotes God's attitude towards us, but grace describes His power at work in us for our salvation.

Grace is more than God helping us to avoid damaging decisions that lead us to destructive places. Grace overcomes the power of destructive addiction. What we cannot possibly stop doing, grace stops in its tracks. But grace is more than just a counteractive force to addiction. It refines and sculpts our living souls so that wholeness radiates out of us. It changes our inner desires from wanting but resisting *sin in me* choices to not wanting to comfort oneself with *sin in me* choices at all. Mind you, this is not the result of a program that you will work through; it is the outcome of trusting God to do in you what you cannot do for yourself no matter how hard you try. What comes into play with grace is what is called the "great exchange."

In Galatians 5, Paul gives us an abbreviated glimpse of the kinds of symptoms people get caught up in, calling them "acts of the sinful nature" (see Galatians 5:19-21 for a full catalog). Then he tells us the good news, that those who keep in step with the Spirit see fruit replacing these symptoms—love, joy peace, patience, kindness, goodness, faithfulness, gentleness, and self-control. These are what the great exchange is all about. As the empowering presence of the Spirit produces transformation in our lives, the *sin in me* is replaced with the fruit of the Spirit. You know you are progressing when you— and others, especially your family—begin to see these characteristics growing in your life. What grace ultimately accomplishes in us is to refit us for the Garden. Grace acts to reverse the effects of the Fall.

To put it another way, mercy is what happens when a murderer is pardoned out of prison. Mercy also is displayed when that murderer has been taken into the family of the person he robbed of life, even to the point of being adopted as a son. But mercy cannot make that man good or change his desires when another relationship goes sour and his anger pushes him to rub out a life yet again. It is the work of grace that empowers him to shed his murderous heart, to lose the desire for revenge, and to become a peace-filled person. Only by God actively working by His grace inside this man's heart does real transformation, into becoming the son he was adopted to be, take place.

You can see this difference between mercy and grace in the latter half of 1 John 1:9. As we confess our sins, God is *faithful and just to forgive our sins* (mercy) and *to cleanse us from all unrighteousness* (grace). The forgiving and the cleansing are diverse works of God in our lives, both absolutely necessary and yet different. We do not get grace because we are obedient; we get it because we could not be obedient without it. Grace enables our obedience as we trust Him. All you have to do is take hold of what God has already given you. I will explain this further when we reach the subject of appropriation.

PREACH THE GOSPEL TO YOURSELF

In 1911, the expression "pie in the sky" was first used in a humorous, but sardonic, take-off rendition of the church hymn, "In the Sweet By and By." It referred to the thinking of well-meaning people who concentrated more on how to get others into heaven than on meeting needs their audience was facing daily. Later the phrase came to refer to any prospect of future happiness which was unlikely ever to be realized.

Perhaps you are tempted to think what I have described is pie in the sky. The idea that your damaged soul could be restored and renewed to allow your created self to emerge may seem impossible. You may have thought that all God offered through Jesus was only the hope that when you died you would go to heaven. In the meantime you just had to muddle through life carrying your unfinished business the best you could. Let me state unequivocally that this is the lie that the enemy wants you to hang onto. He lies to us every day. If he can keep you thinking this is pie in the sky, especially on days when the journey to wholeness seems painful and tough, if he can keep you focused on trying to do in your own strength what you are not able to do, then you will quit the journey before you see the healing work of grace in your life.

I sometimes receive those middle-of-the-night counseling calls. People who have heard me teach about unfinished business ask if they can come and talk. Often this means can they come and confess. They sit in my living room and unfold their stories, which are as familiar to me as they are sad: bad choices, financial doom, loss of love in the marriage. I remember asking one man, Jack, when this downhill trend started. Jack mentioned that the marriages of several of his Christian mentors with whom he was close blew apart publicly, permanently. He had a pie-in-the-sky moment. He began thinking at that moment that if these spiritual men could not keep it together, what hope did he have? And so down the same road Jack sped, until the night when, through the tiny voice of a child, God spoke truth into his life.

There is danger in listening to yourself. That's right. Do not for one moment believe that everything that you think, that passes through your mind, that your tongue speaks is really true. Why? Because, it is through your damaged emotions that Satan will lie to you. Your emotions color the world of your mind more than you know. In fact, neither you nor anyone else knows how damaged one's emotions really are. Nor can any of us fathom the continuing wounds aimed at us daily while living in a fallen world.

Here is what I do know—Satan uses our own voice against

us. He allows us to hear ourselves speak the poisonous words as if they originated in us, passing off "I want to..." or "I fear..." or "I know..." statements with impunity. We actually believe we are speaking the truth when we hear ourselves talking. So you might say, "There is no hope for me," in denial of the real hope that is within you, and believe it. Or say that failing to control your sin choices is inevitable, even while ignoring that He who is in you is greater than he who is in the world! Or that your marriage is over. Or that you are just being true to your principles, when you really are being prideful. Or that you cannot change. Any number of lies can fall from your lips. The moment we begin to believe our every thought and word is always true truth, we are already halfway down the journey towards fear and damage.

You will probably need help here. You may not be hearing yourself clearly because you have said the same lies so often that they fit you as normally and comfortably as your socks. Or your most recent wound is pulsating so hard on your soul's nerves that the ghost of a former addiction has raised its ugly head again in your life, begging to be reinstated. Having someone you can trust challenge the lies may be life-saving. But rescue from the lies is not just knowing there are lies coming out of your mouth.

Instead of listening to yourself, you need to preach the good news of Jesus to yourself. The lies of the enemy are often only recognized as such when the truth of gospel appears. This may seem self-evident, but emotional lies are very powerful. They can take control of your decision-making will. Therefore you cannot let a day go by when you do not rehearse the truth of the gospel to yourself. This truth is what opens us to God, keeping us from the slippery slope of empty comfort choices from among the seven deadly sins.

What is this gospel—in practical terms—that we need to hear every day? It starts with the truth that God is in the process of conforming you into the image of His Son, Jesus (Romans 8:29). You are on a journey to be changed into His likeness. It continues with the truth that God is using all that has happened to you as a part of this process, even the bad stuff (Romans 8:28). Not just the tragedies and triumphs in your current life, but all that has happened to you since the day you were born, even the parts you do not want to remember. These truths are accomplished in our lives through the cross and the resurrection (Colossians 2:9-15).

Add to this that God has already given you everything you need for life and godliness through your knowledge of Him who called you by His own glory and goodness (2 Peter 1:3). And that God's grace (His empowering presence) has appeared to you, teaching you to say "No" to ungodliness and worldly passions and to live a self-controlled, upright, and godly life in the time you have to live (Titus 2:11-12). These verses are not merely great Sunday school memorization fodder, they speak deep truth against the dark lies you toy around with in your soul.

And these are the truths I often share with people who know them already but are ignoring their potency. I have pointed out to them how easily they had eaten the elephant. Jack, the man I mentioned earlier, had fallen to one of the all-time great schemes of the enemy—to judge the strength of God's power at work in him by the failed performance of others. I reminded him that his relationship with God was between him and God alone. The choices of another cannot be allowed to harm that relationship. And so it is with all of us. Preaching the gospel to yourself is the spiritual antidote to Satan's ruinous schemes. Paraphrasing Paul in 2 Timothy 3:14, you will continue to live out what you are *convinced of*—even when damaged emotions say otherwise—and even when others do not.

SO WHO AM I ANYWAY?

I started this chapter talking about stuck identity. This is the mask you and I were wearing before grace got hold of us. You may still be hiding behind this devil-may-care façade long since you have come under the loving reign of Jesus, believing this is who you really are. The truth I want you to take away is that this is not who you are and does not reflect your created self, no matter how many years you continue to parade along as if it were.

When you place your faith in Jesus and are moved from

the dark kingdom into his Kingdom of light, you receive a new identity. This is not a live-along-side-the-old-identity. Nor is it a competing identity. It is a replacement identity—a restored identity. It is the identity you were always meant to have, had sin never infected you. This new identity is "child of God" (1 John 3:1). This identity denotes a distinct break from your human past.

The Bible covers the history of man from the creative work of God in Genesis to the re-creative acts of God at the end of the age. All humans are the descendants of Adam. Biologically, all the people who have lived on the earth since the beginning of time were genetically present in the first couple. When they rebelled, the whole human race was there involved in their decision. The biblical shorthand for this is being "in Adam." It literally means you are a product of Adam—and not just in your DNA. Your stuck identity was also shaped by the aftereffects of Adam's disastrous decision, which was the Fall. You chose sin to comfort your hurting heart because it was as natural as breathing. This is what it means to be in Adam.

But something extraordinary happened when you put your faith in Jesus. God, in saving you, placed you "in Christ." Paul uses this truth over and over again in his writings to express your new reality. Before, you were under the absolute reign of depravity. Now you are free—it is for freedom that Jesus set us free (Galatians 5:1). "In Christ" defines your new identity as

God's child. Whatever Jesus is, is what you are now. And Jesus is the last Adam (1 Corinthians 15:45). This means that Jesus is the final act Adam as Adam was meant to be, but did not become because of his act of rebellion. This characterization of Jesus is what Paul had in mind in Romans 8:29. You are not predestined to be conformed to Jesus as God the Son—an impossibility—but conformed to Jesus the last Adam, a complete human in tune with the Father, the creation, and all others. Jesus, the perfect human, is a picture of your created self. This is your true identity. When you look into the eyes of Jesus, you see yourself.

"Christ…is our life!" Paul declares in Colossians 3:3. That statement is stuffed with meaning. But rather than dissect it to the nth degree, let me just say that if you have been confused about what your identity is supposed to be, *Jesus* is it. But do not worry if you do not get your head around it the first time, or even the hundredth time, because none of us can fully grasp the whole of it. John assures us, however, that even if what we are to become has not been fully made known, when Jesus finally shows up again we will be like him because we will see him as he really is (1 John 3:2).

Transformation is about your progress toward your true identity. As you transform, who you really are emerges. This created self has been covered in layers of damaging choices as well as the good deeds done in the mistaken belief that you could reform yourself. The good news is that Jesus on the cross became sin for us so that we might become the righteousness of God (2 Corinthians 5:21). He took it upon Himself to restore what was broken in us yesterday, today, and tomorrow. Wherever your identity is stuck, he has already erased its power over you. You may not know this, but it is still true.

How you think about this truth does matter though. Your whole life has been about seeing yourself through the lies of your damaged emotions. They will continue to lie to you. They pull you towards sticking with the stuck identity. Your damaged emotions will shape your view of reality. Even though it is a false view, you will act as if it is true. Transforming involves the renewing of your mind (Romans 12:2). The essence of a renewed mind is having a mind that recognizes and embraces truth over lies and aligns one's actions according to the truth.

Here is a simple three-step process to practice when you realize your damaged emotions are lying to you. First, identify it as a lie. Say "That is a lie!" out loud so you can stop it in its tracks. Recognize where that lie came from. Now, the lie may have its human origins in some person who wounded you...knighted you with names that are demeaning...or even "lovingly" rocked your world. Or the lies might have popped up in your head unbidden. You made a judgment on someone. You made a judgment on yourself. You felt the tug of a temptation to act in a destructive way. But its source is still Satan, and you need to say so. He may have used your voice, but he conceived the lie all the same. "Satan hatched that lie in me!" Lying is, after all, his language.

The second step is to replace the lie with God's truth about your created identity. In other words, *speak the truth.* "Here is what God has said. This is what is true." You may actually have to do this in the face of feelings that are rebelling against what you are saying. You might want at that moment to choose *sin in me* as a comfort to the pain of the lie. Instead, you should say, "Although there is sin in me offering to comfort me, I am in God's presence at this very moment. He has already given me all the mercy and grace I need for life and godliness. I trust the healing power of His provision over the comfort choice I would make." This is the practical way the gospel is applied to what can be renewed by God alone.

Finally, take faith steps empowered by grace and live in the truth. This means that from here on out you are trusting God's truth about Him and you more than the lies of the enemy. What you are not asked to do by God is to fake it until it becomes true. If you have made *sin in me* choices, repent. If you have damaged others by your actions, apologize and reconcile. But do not live trapped any longer. What God has said is true. Moreover, the power to live the truth has been given. Move on!

It may seem unreal but it is the realest action you will ever take. You will find if you do this in time your damaged emotions will heal and no longer have the power to tell you such lies about yourself. Your rational thoughts, now renewed by God, will begin to balance out your emotions in the life-decision function of the heart. You will make decisions others see as wise and healthy, rather than irrational as they were when your heart was under the control of your damaged emotions.

It is critical that you do not rely on your own strength in this three-step process. You do not have the ability to change your mind about the lie or to heal the damaged emotions behind it. But for you to come to trust God's strength in this process, you are going to have to move towards Him in intimacy. This will make sense. Keep reading…

7. TRANSFORMATION

TRANSFORMATION IS GOD'S WORK.

You are not being invited to start a self-help project. You cannot fix yourself because you did not make yourself. None of us did. What we did do as humans is mess ourselves up, and now we have no idea how to put the pieces back into place. What each of us has to accept is that only God can fix what is messed up. God thought you up and He alone knows what He created you to be. He alone has the power to restore you to that creation.

Satan is counting on us swallowing the lie that failure on our part to make ourselves whole at any point means we are out. No use to go on because we blew the chance we had. Honestly, no matter how many times you have failed in strength, God waits for you to be with Him so He can display His strength in transforming you. This is the whole point of what the Bible calls "sanctification." This word is about the life we lead between the time we placed our faith in Jesus and the time when we will finally stand in God's very presence. When we believed, we were saved from the penalty of sin. When we are finally with God, we will be saved from the presence of sin. Right now, we are being sanctified, which means we are being saved from the power of sin. Log that away into your thinking for the days when the enemy lies to you. You still may not have the ability to be good for God. But you now have His very presence in you in the Holy Spirit, who is more than just a casual passenger as you carry on your life. It is not you who are saving yourself from the power of sin—how absurd and impossible. No, it is God who does that for you as you trustingly lean into Him.

Furthermore, transformation is not *your* goal. It's God's goal for you. Jesus said the point of eternal *zoe* was that we may know God (John 17:3). Your personal goal is to know and enjoy God. Being made whole is always an outcome of deepening your relationship with Him. Mike Yaconelli put it this way in his book *Messy Spirituality*: "The way of the spiritual life begins where we are now in the mess of our lives. Accepting the reality of our broken, flawed life is the beginning of spirituality, not because the spiritual life will remove our flaws, but because we let go of seeking perfection and instead seek God, the one who is present in the tangledness of our lives."[7]

Why pursuing deep relationship with God is so important is because Satan's final line of attack to keep us from getting well is to focus our attention on fighting to get well instead of on knowing God. As we see what the problem is, his lie is to encourage us to go after it in a misguided belief that resisting the *sin in me* choices or even healing the *hurt of the heart* is something which we must personally manage. This is misdirection on a scale greater than that of the magician David Copperfield. We cannot fight our way to spiritual health. Never could. Never will. Paul records that the point when he realized his own weakness in being unable to change himself was when God's promised grace became effective in him (2 Corinthians 12:9).This is why he boasted in his weaknesses, so that he could see God do in him what he could not do for himself. Essentially, when we focus on the problem, we find we have no attention left for the One who delivers and heals.

Healing is found in intimacy with God. And when God heals the *hurt of the heart* in us, the *sin in me* has nothing it can hook into. It no longer offers us anything we need. Then we find that our symptoms disappear of their own accord. Reread that last statement. This is what being with God does in transformation. The symptoms dissipate as we deepen our healing relationship with God.

This is not Devotions 101. It is not a call to more Bible study and prayer. If you are teetering on the brink of spiritual meltdown, you certainly would not find that counsel helpful or hopeful. Why? Because it is about doing more stuff for God and you are already tired out from trying. What I am counseling is spiritual rest in its place. It is about being with God in the way Adam and Eve strolled with Him every evening in the Garden. It is about receiving love and power from Him instead of begging for Him to give you stuff you have already been granted just because you belong to Him.

BEING WITH GOD WITHOUT AN AGENDA

How close are you to self-destruction? I do not ask this flippantly. Many people live on the edge for a long time before their lives unravel for all to see. You may have unfinished business that is not as ripe as that of those who have already fallen over the edge, but it lives and will bite in time if left to itself.

If you want to be freed from the hidden destructive forces that are building in your life, you will need to practice certain spiritual disciplines. Now, do not judge this statement until you have read the rest of the chapter. I know a problem in the Church is that we have turned the spiritual disciplines on their head and teach people a backwards way of attaining a spiritual walk with God through hard work. Where we need to start in building our deeper relationship is by practicing rest. But before I talk about rest as the first spiritual of discipline leading to intimacy, let Ephesians capture your attention.

If you think about Ephesians, you will realize Paul is speaking to believers he has not personally met, those whose faith he has only heard about (1:15). The flow of the letter is to give these believers the basics they need to grow in this faith. For three chapters he paints the picture of what God has gloriously done through Christ and in them – seating them in Christ at His right hand (2:6). In chapters 4 and 5 he challenges them on how to walk in their faith. He concludes in chapter 6 with how to stand in the face of spiritual warfare. Watchman

Nee called this understanding of Ephesians: "sit…walk…stand."

Consider how important it is for Paul to have given half of the letter over to what God has done for those He chose "in Christ before the creation of the world to be holy and blameless in His sight." Paul's starting point in living as a believer is not a call to action, but a call to start by contemplating what God has done in Christ for us. He uses words like redemption, glory, mercy, grace, peace, mystery, power, and love to describe how God transforms us. So shortly into the letter, Paul speaks of several significant things he has asked God for on their behalf. In 1:17, Paul prays an *intimacy* prayer—that his readers would be given the Spirit of wisdom and revelation so that they would know God better. This is a significant prayer because Paul knows they will not move forward in becoming spiritually whole without a growing relationship with God that is brought about by the Spirit instead of more Bible study and prayer.

The word "know" loses its force when it lands in English. For us, know is an educational word. We go to school to learn and know about various subjects. But Paul, in his language, is using a word that is much richer. It carries the idea of knowledge gained by encountering God, knowing Him in the way that speaks of experience. You can study space exploration and know all about rockets and the moon. But Neil Armstrong, as the first to stand on it, knows the moon. He has experienced the giant leap of being there. This is the point of Paul's prayer—that you come to really know God intimately— not through education—but by being drawn to experience Him. This prayer is for you as well. Only when you know God better will you get well. Meaning you will healed and delivered.

What if I told you that prayer and Bible study are disciplines that come into play in the middle of Ephesians? They are the 'do' disciplines. But their power—and our ability to even stay interested in them—is found in the practice first of the 'done' disciplines. *Done* disciplines are those practices which open us up to receive from God all He has done through the death and resurrection of Jesus. They are about being filled by God Himself. *Do* disciplines are what we do (such as fasting and prayer) to supplement our faith, growing in the character of Jesus so we will be useful for his Kingdom instead of fruitless and frustrated (2 Peter 1:5-9).

Rest is a done discipline. Rest from our own work; rest in His strength; rest in His presence; rest that allows us to understand what we have received. Rest as a spiritual discipline is about stopping our trying—stopping, period, and just being with God. It is allowing ourselves to hear how He loves and accepts us before we try any heavy lifting. In fact, it is in rest that we find God is the One who has already done all the heavy lifting. He invites us to find this out by being with Him quietly, reflectively, receptively.

Rest refutes our personal self-talk. One of our greatest

needs is to rest from judging ourselves; from beating ourselves up internally; from saving the enemy work by believing the worst about ourselves—without resting in God's delight to have us as His child. If I know anything, I know we are very susceptible to embracing the accusing lies of the enemy and repeat them foolishly to ourselves. "I am weak. I am unable to be good. I am unable to stop repeating addictive sin. I am hopeless, useless, and worthless to God." Or, "I can do this. I am good at being holy. I am spiritually powerful." This also is the enemy speaking. When we rest, we hear the true words of God about ourselves; that He always knew we are foolish and unable, but we will be changed by His presence and power. He has not abandoned us.

Paul says we are "accepted in the Beloved" (Eph. 1:6). The King James Version captures the reality of God's "gracing us" in this beautiful word picture of us, God the Father, and Jesus. This is what we hear when we start resting. We hear the Father telling us what worth He has placed on us and where He has placed us—not just our cleaned up, righteous self, but the still messed up, untransformed self we are when He redeemed us. But if we are to escape further damage of the unfinished business of our lives, we need rest so we can have our minds renewed in this way:

- I have no strength of my own to beat what defeats me, but I am safe within Christ.
- I have no personal resources to fix myself, but God already

knows this and accepts me.

- My agenda is to be with God, not to first prepare myself to be with Him.

- I do not have to clean up to be in God's presence, although this goes against the grain.

- I do not need to hide anything, since God already knows everything.

- I need to stop explaining things to God and to start receiving from God.

If you never have spiritually rested, you may not know how to do this. Rest is being with God without an agenda. It means being ready to listen and hear what God has for you—mercy, grace, love, restoration. You may pray or read Scripture while you are with Him, but that rest is unstructured time with Him, allowing Him to guide you and reveal to you His desires for you. This is about building a personal relationship with God.

Here is a first step that you will find simple, yet challenging. Meditate on Hebrews 4:16 in God's company. Recognize that you are coming into your *Abba*'s presence (*Abba* means 'Daddy' Gal. 4:6) and are there to receive mercy and grace—the elements of His great love for you. Allow the Spirit to empower you to listen for His words of acceptance and affirmation for you. It would do you well to review Paul's own experience with this recorded in 2 Corinthians 12, especially verse 9. Do this every day as you start the morning, even if it is only for sixty seconds. Do not ask for anything, just receive what he wants to give. Rest on His power to remake your life and renew your mind. In time, you may come to practice this discipline throughout your day. As you attune your life to knowing you are accepted in the Beloved, you will find you are struggling less with the power of the *sin in me*. This is the power of rest. This is the stuff of building intimacy with your Daddy.

For you who are willing to engage with God in a ruthless searching process, the revealed specter of the sin of your heart (anger, lust, greed, envy, sloth, gluttony, pride) may scare you and seem to you more powerful than the practice of rest. We are much like kindergartners who cannot grasp the need for naptime at school. The sad part of all this is that you might not consistently take the time to get what you really need because you will not value rest. Rest is transformational. To be with God undemandingly, with no resources of our own, is the most potent antidote for such a destructive presence in our souls. As counterintuitive as this may seem, doing nothing in our own strength to save ourselves from the power of sin is doing the most we can possibly do in the process of becoming the person we were created to be by God.

You will not grow in your ability to rest by a quick session or two with God. Being with God without an agenda—but instead to hear and receive from Him—has a learning curve. You have to *make* time intentionally. You will never *find* time for this! You will have to get away from distractions. Here are some practical steps that can enhance your practice of rest time with God:

- Go where you are physically comfortable while you are with God.

- It is good to tell God what you want from Him—peace, grace, mercy, etc.

- Read Scripture for the purpose of hearing God to speak to you.

- Review your day with God and acknowledge His presence during that day.

- Make being alone with God a regular part of your life.

It may take months before you begin to sense you truly are ready to hear God when you are with Him. Why? Because we have busy minds. Instead of the ability to listen in quiet, we have cultivated a brain geared to short bursts of focus and multitasking. But do not give up this means of pursuing God. He is already there and ready for you to know Him better. He has also given you His Spirit so this can be real in your life. Practice. Listen. Wait. Rest. In time, as you do this consistently, you will begin to have the kind of relationship with God you have always wanted, and more.

APPROPRIATING WHAT YOU HAVE ALREADY

When I said "to be with God with no resources," I am speaking about *our* personal stockpile, not God's. A further prayer by Paul in Ephesians 1:18 asked God to show his readers the wonders of His supply for all they needed. He had alluded to this in 1:3 when he blessed God for blessing His people with every spiritual blessing in Christ. When I teach on this, I ask people, "How many blessings has God given us?" "All," they usually respond. "Has He withheld anything that you will have to ask for later?" "No," they admit. Why is this interaction so important for those I mentor? Because so often when we are at our wit's end over the unfinished business of our lives, we find ourselves asking God for spiritual stuff as if our cupboard is bare. You know you have. I know I have.

Paul's request for them is an *appropriation* prayer. "You guys need God to open your eyes to what you have." He speaks of the hope upon which believers can stake their future, the riches of His glorious inheritance in his children, and God's immeasurable power. It is not unusual for people to think of seeing the hope, riches, and power at a distance like a goal to be reached somehow, or a treasure room to one day enter somewhere in heaven. But these resources are already in our souls, placed there by an intimate, loving God who knows our need better than we do ourselves. Gaining understanding about these assets is not merely to set our minds at ease; they are there as the resources for our transformational journey. So if rest is the first "done" discipline that we practice in order that we might move towards spiritual wholeness, appropriation is the second.

What is appropriation? In my home we have a refrigerator in which everything is fair game. The other day I stowed a left over meal there when I returned from a long day on the road. And then I told my wife I knew it would be eaten by our live-at-home son. Sure enough, the container was empty in the morning. My son, who knows that all food is available in the refrigerator, claimed it as a midnight snack. This is appropriation—freely taking what is there for you without hesitation. No begging. No fear. Your need filled at the moment you reach out to take. I cannot tell you how much this powerful discipline has freed me from one addictive sin after another over time.

When I first entered into this transformational process with God, I had numerous symptoms. I was deeply addicted to a number of sinful actions, some of which were already painfully in the process of destroying me. One actively was sucking time and intimacy out of my relationship with my wife, Shirley. And though I knew this, I could not stop. I was addicted. It controlled me. Then I began appropriating the power that God had given me. I did not have much faith—I later laughingly called it my five-minute faith steps in this process of appropriation. Every five minutes the addiction would hijack my damaged emotions to demand its way with me. But then I would go back to the bottomless supply of God's power and appropriate. For another five minutes. Then it became ten minutes. Then half an hour, a day, a week, months of faith appropriation. Then the addiction released its grip on me, and I was free for the first time in years. Not because I fought it with my strength. I had failed miserably trying that routine in the past. The most I had achieved that way was to become, in twelve steps parlance, a "dry drunk." I wasn't actively acting on my addiction but I sure wanted to. Through appropriation, not only was I not acting on my addiction, it no longer controlled my desires. Yet I know I would have never been freed in this and other areas if I had not been willing to admit my need and take what I needed from what God had already given me for this very purpose.

Perhaps you feel this spiritual discipline is not necessary because you're purposefully oblivious to how bad things really are going inside you. Miles Stanford wrote years ago, "In order to appropriate something for our daily walk in Christ, there are two essentials: to see what is already ours in Christ and to be aware of our need for it."[8] What I see holding so many people back from experiencing freedom from unfinished business is our failure to admit our need, rather than any lack in supply. It is our decision to avoid self-awareness that leaves us hopeless and open to the lies of the enemy that the *sin in me* is our only comfort.

Look closer at the four reasons we do not feel the need for appropriation and see if you can discern the reason for your own hesitation.

- You have not yet grown tired of the false relief you think you are getting from your addictive sin. You still feel empowered in anger, justified in comments prompted by envy, sated in the appetite gluttony is feeding, or whatever form the pleasure of sin has taken in your private world. You will need God to bring you to crisis before you see the need.

- You are not aware of what you have in Christ in practical ways. Experientially, God's hope, riches, and power are merely Bible study fodder to you, not your spiritual reality. I have seen this often and believe it is the result of poor discipleship—a void in a believer's growth process due to churches making more important the 'do' disciplines rather than the 'done' work of God. While you may feel your need, you still will have to deepen your trust in God's presence with you through rest before His supply becomes real to you. Remember that one of the enemy's lies is to tell you that you are alone. Rest and appropriation are interconnected in Ephesians, and in real life too.

- You are still investing deeply in the blame game. Revenge, hurt, or exposure of the guilty—as well as self-pity and helplessness for yourself—are your goals, not spiritual wholeness. You may not be willing to admit this, but it is true. You will not feel your need until you ask God to ruthlessly search your heart.

- Your addiction is too great in your eyes to believe any freedom is possible. This is a lie of Satan, and moving forward will require help from a spiritual community.

Why should the discipline of appropriation be important for you? Like the rest of us, you have failed by trying to deal with your unfinished business using your own resources. Face it. *You* have nothing that works. If you continue to ignore this discipline, in time the lid will blow off of your unfinished business. But because of the good news of Jesus Christ, destruction and defeat do not need to be your future story. Take what is yours already. Move forward in wholeness with God, empowered by the resources you have been given.

TRANSFORMED THROUGH MEDITATION ON GOD'S LOVE

What I am about to describe next may seem obvious to you, but it needs to be remembered as often as possible. The single most critical factor in healing your unfinished business is the love of God. The personal grip of His love is our greatest security in this alarming process of transformation. It is the only thing that opens the door to the renewing of our mind and to our being able to rest in Him.

God's love is something we know theologically, theoretically, but often not really, not convincingly. Not enough to sustain us daily with the feeling that we are safe. Deep down in our honest selves, where no one can see, most of us are feeling extremely unsafe and unsure of our welcome by God. We realize the walled-off sections of our soul where sin lurks are not really hidden. So we wait for…what? Judgment to fall? To be exposed and censured? A chance to plead our case? God to own up to His failures? Unasked for forgiveness, as if that was likely? The fact is we are uncertain of our relationship with God, even though our official theology says He is Love.

This is why the lies of the enemy seem so much more real than the truth of God. Satan suggests that the *sin in me* will make us safer. In a perverse way we grab hold of sin because we feel like it leaves us in charge, in control—and find in the end that we bought into a very bad lie. But by then the love of God seems too far away from us, too elusive for us to trust. We expect that God is disgusted—even angry beyond forgiveness—with us and our mess. Unthinkingly we have bought into the lie that God is unsafe, and now as far as love goes, untrustworthy. We find ourselves with no alternative, stuck on a terrible ride to the death.

Years ago Gerald May wrote a powerful book called *Addiction and Grace*. His picture of the constancy of God's love is worth special consideration for all of us who are looking for a station where we can disembark from our destructive journey. He wrote: *"God's love is more constant than human love can be. Human loving has its pure moments and parental love especially can sometimes express a likeness of God in its deep steadiness. But however solid it may be, human love is always prey to selfishness and distractions bred by attachment...It is not so with God's love. God goes on loving us regardless of who we are or what we do. This does not mean God is like a permissive human parent who makes excuses and ignores the consequences of a child's behavior. In God's constantly respectful love, consequences of our actions are very real, and they can be horrible, and we are responsible. We are even responsible for the compulsive behaviors of our addictions. The freedom God preserves in us has a double edge. On the one hand, it means God's love and empowerment are always with us. On the other, it means there is no authentic escape from the truth of our choices. But even when our choices are destructive and their consequences are hurtful, God's love remains unwavering."* [9]

For your true journey of being conformed to Jesus' image, you must have a daily knowing of this changeless love. In Ephesians 3:14-19, Paul prays a *transformational* prayer for his readers, that they would be filled with power and grasp the love of Christ. The first half of the request is about grace. Paul is asking on their behalf that the empowering presence of the Spirit would change the nature of their hearts—the place where life decisions are made. The heart is where people, including you and me, go off the tracks, choosing sin to comfort our hurt. Paul sees that they need power beyond the self-help variety— that they would realize Christ's very presence, who is able to transform them because He is far stronger than the sin that has been having its way with them.

But there is more. Paul also lasers in on their need for understanding a love that is so beyond them it is humanly incomprehensible. Yet understanding it is the necessary ingredient for being filled with the full measure of God. Grasping this love has been made possible because they—and now, we—have the mind of Christ. His love is what brings us to trust the safeness of God in the middle of our mess when we are anything but whole and clean. God loves the fearful, broken, hateful, deceitful parts of ourselves as well as the presentable in-order parts. It gives us hope that we will see the end of our unfinished business when no end seems in sight. There is nothing we can do that will make God love us more. There is nothing we can do that will make God love us less. This truth anchors our future.

We secretly want to believe this is true even when our emotions are lying to us that it can never be. Perhaps the problem starts with the way we have framed our understanding of His love. We have relied on the Bible's report of it alone. "Jesus loves me this I know, for the Bible tells me so," is not enough. This is the "know" of Paul's third prayer: "and to know this love that surpasses knowledge" (3:19). He prays that we get to the place of encountering this incredible love of God so that we will know and not doubt it as we do so many other loves we have felt or seen. Know it possessed us even when we were outside God's family. Know this love will never run short for us.

So what will you do about your need for this truth? How you think about God's love will affect whether or not you will ask Him for healing and deliverance. Here is another "done" discipline I have found powerful in the transformational process God is carrying me through. It is the practice of meditating on God's love. Meditating is the process in which we grasp the truth of God's love. How deep is it? How wide is it? How high and long does it stretch? This meditation offers a daily reminder to me of who I am to Him. I actually say out loud while I am in His presence, "I know you love me. I am safe." I hear Him affirm this in my heart, even on days when my wounded emotions are raw and I feel the beckoning of the *sin in me*—especially on those days.

INTIMACY LEADS TO DEEPENING TRUST

I have noticed that many people who grapple with woundedness ask questions like, "Why did this happen to me?" or "Why did God let this happen?" Most times these questions cannot be answered this side of the grave. But I can tell you that one of the outcomes of pursuing intimacy with God is deepening trust. And it takes a deeper trust in God to allow Him to heal and deliver. However, if you choose to invest in the relationship God offers, you will find your unanswered questions are not as important as the way God uses all the events of your life, including the bad and ugly ones you struggle with, to bring about wholeness in you.

Trust builds because you will begin to know God in a personal way. You will spend time hanging out with Him, letting Him speak love to you, learning His path for you. It will lead to confidence in your relationship with Him. I have a son who understands the idea of confidence in his relationship with me. The other day he was not getting out of the house fast enough for us to get to our destination in time (we were already late) to meet up with his mom, so I fussed at him loudly. After we finally settled into our seats at the end of the journey, my wife perceived that he was upset with me for how I had talked to him. After we were in a place where we could talk, he started the conversation by telling me he had already forgiven me. I thought that was the end of the conversation. But then he added, "But you haven't offered an apology yet." I laughed and apologized. It was a typical exchange for him and me. He is free to say what he thinks, knowing I will accept his words without anger or rejection. This is trust.

It is this kind of trust intimacy with God produces. You will find you can say anything—you can confess sin, can admit temptations are attractive, ask hard questions, wish for a different life, be honest about being angry with Him,—without fearing a mortal blow to the relationship. You find you are finally safe to be yourself before Him, because He welcomes such honesty. He is like no earthly parent you have ever had. He is the supreme Father who knew you could not become all you were created to be without His power. He knows your unfinished business better than you do, yet there is no condemnation in Him.

Trust addresses an attitude in us which Larry Crabb calls demandingness. Demandingness is just that, our insistent demanding that God follow our plan in the transformational process. It is an attempt at human command. Because a person pursues a deepening relationship with God, that person thinks he or she can set up the outcome of the process. His or her lack of any real knowing of God drives this grab for control.

But demandingness is often masked as spiritual expectancy. "I draw close to God, and He supplies all my needs…" with the unexpressed addendum "…as I define them." This is just another form of the obedience model of living. It causes people to get mad at God. They have assumed that what they want for themselves is what God wants. They think that if they follow the process, they will get what they expect when they get far enough down the healing journey. Their desires seem so reasonable and even spiritual to them. So when God shows no sign of granting the promises they thought they were working towards, things get ugly. People have been known to fall into bitterness. Others quit on God altogether and go back to the way of life that was destroying them.

In a human sense, this is understandable. How do you explain to the man who is trying to follow Jesus and still after months cannot land a job that pays a living wage so he can take care of his family that yes, God is at work in his life? How can you answer the woman whose husband abandoned her and her child that no, God is making no promise that the man will return even though she has stayed faithful? The why of these situations cannot be explained, but the faithfulness of God, even when you do not see Him working, is always real.

Demandingness is the appeal of the hurting. Those who utilize its services see the promises of God in black and white. In their minds, God is only true if He does their personal version of His promises. This kind of thinking is akin to the naughty and nice list of Santa Claus. "Since I am on the nice list, I have a right to the presents I wished for." For God not to produce on command is to forfeit His place in their lives.

But those who grow in intimacy with God will come to realize He loves you more deeply and knows what paths you will need to walk in the process of becoming whole. This is not the easy road, nor will it always make sense to you. You come to learn that His knowledge about what is good for you is infinite, while discovering that your plans are shortsighted due to your human limitations. Trusting Him on this may be at first tough to swallow. Sometimes you will cry out in pain. What will get you through the pain is your confidence in the relationship. Trust means you discover that on the high-risk-wire act called life, there is no other net that will catch you but His. God may not give you all you thought was yours. He probably will not tell you why. But only those who pursue intimacy will become what they were created to be. And that in itself is what produces your trust in Him.

INTIMACY LEADS TO GAINING HOPE

The other byproduct of intimacy is hope. I clearly remember my life before entering a transformational process with God, so I understand hopelessness. While I was coexisting with my unfinished business, I twisted in the wind with anxiety that nothing would ever get better, all the while trying harder to make myself better. The emotional toll of hopelessness can make one afraid of God due to the shame that person feels. Shame produces a thought line like this: "I am supposed to be a better person because I trusted in Jesus. So why am I not? It must be something I am not doing right. I seem to be the only one in my church who is not getting it right. God cannot be pleased with me for failing to take His command to be holy as He is holy seriously." The weight of this kind of thinking is on us in our minds and so is the misery of no hope. For those of you who practice the obedience model at a high level, hopelessness may be late in arriving at your party, but it will show up someday with the same pitchforks that pierce the troubled conscience of the less adept.

Intimacy with God delivers hope. And joy. Instead of the feeling that God is looking judgmentally over your shoulder, you find God is lovingly participating in the process with you. Through intimacy we discover God's unstinting acceptance of the responsibility to transform us into what we were created to be. No more of you having to set up fences to hold back your evil desires. A deep relationship with God will change your desires. Paul calls this "hope of the glory of God," something you did not have a snowball's chance in hell for before you placed your faith in Jesus (Romans 5:2).

Hope is restorative. And hope is the pathway out of self-deception, which is a psychological mechanism to protect ourselves from the pain of our stuck self. This self-deceit allows us to live almost unconsciously of that which is damaged and destructive within us. Although we may try to fool ourselves that we're okay when were *not* okay, God certainly is not fooled. Yet He loves us even though we have fearful, broken, hateful, devious parts, as well as what we consider acceptable components.

What we discover in intimacy is that we no longer have need for internal defenses to protect ourselves from the truth. This also takes some healing by God, because our internal self-deception is on autopilot. As soon as an inconvenient truth pops up into our life, our defenses go to work to screen it from view. Self-deception may make it possible for us to live with ourselves, but it never heals us. Intimacy, through rest, appropriation, and meditating on God's love, ends the need for hiding truth about ourselves. We find hope in bringing our brokenness to God because we come to know the reality of both His love for us and His power to transform us. We find that He uses whatever our unfinished business is to move us forward. We are not stuck.

If it takes us some time to respond with trust to His

prompting, the good news is that He will continue to prompt until we get to where He is leading us. He never gets tired and quits on us. This is something you need to store firmly in your mind, because you will hear people who should know better tell you this just ain't so.

Intimacy holds us to the journey that we have to walk. No set of religious rules can do that. Just saying "No" to sin will not keep us on course. Nor will the help of an accountability partner prevent you from going back. At some point, the point of the rules becomes fuzzy and the inner strength to resist sin weakens. Accountability can be gotten around. Transformation is a personal walk, and it requires a Person to make the path straight for us in order to keep on. Intimacy assures us that He will become your most prized friend. That friendship will bring you to spiritual health in ways no other mechanism can. Prizing Him is what will hold us when the delights of sin pressure our damaged emotions with the cheap and useless ways of comfort.

8. COMMUNITY

You Are Not Meant To Travel This Journey Alone.

The most daunting part of the journey to spiritual health is abandoning the secrecy of your unfinished business. I say daunting because this is the place where many people decide the road to spiritual health is too treacherous. Maybe it is because they have been betrayed by wagging tongues and unyielding legalism in the past. Trust was betrayed. They saw no understanding where there was supposed to be humility and humanity—and restoration. These damaged souls have unfortunately come to believe that the secrets inside them are safer while they are hidden away, not when they are revealed. Their experiences are tragic and should never have happened. It is not hard to comprehend why people like you and me want to keep our unfinished business a secret to ourselves.

But secret-keeping is exactly what we cannot do. Not forever. For at the worst possible moment, secrets steal out and destroy. Moreover, it is secrecy that gives the comfort activity you have chosen (letting the *sin in me* soothe the *hurt of the heart*) its growing power. The lie becomes stronger. The addiction hooks in deeper. The fissures in your soul begin to take on alarming aspects as your damaged emotions start being harmed by your own actions. It is your choice to go it alone that puts you firmly into a maze with no exits, always seeking the way out but continually running into dead ends.

Some of you already have left your faith communities over your secret-keeping. Your leaving was probably not for the reasons you put out for public consumption. You may have felt you would be condemned. Or you blamed them for the pain you are grappling with. Or you may sense that once your story is out you would become a second-class member and you would never be able to regain the respect and love of your community. You might believe that going somewhere else will give you a chance to start over again as an equal. Or that going nowhere at all is for the best. Leaving also may have allowed you to indulge in the full potency of your addiction.

If this defines your experience, or you are thinking through an exit strategy for yourself, take this caution to heart. What you imagine the people of your community will think of you may only be your pain talking. We are all self-protecting creatures. When we hurt, we often are petty and ready to believe people are criticizing us when no one is. You might find it easy to condemn those who love you when you are in pain because you expect to be hurt by them. Running away to where no one knows you is your perverse way of punishing them. However, it is you that will be punished by your leaving. This tactic leads to a new way of being isolated, since no one in the new community will know you deeply enough to help. You may think you are keeping safe, but it's not reality. What you need most is to engage with people in your current faith community who will help you towards God's healing. This takes humility and courage.

On the other hand, some of you are attending a faith community that is spiritually unhealthy. While no church is without people with messy lives, a whole community of such people suggests unwholesomeness has become the rule rather than the exception. Here is a short list of indicators that the community of which you are a part is in trouble.

- **Blind loyalty** is the preferred mode of belonging. Sin in top leaders is glossed over. No one ever is allowed to hold those who lead accountable, and they become angry if anyone attempts to do so, even in love.

- **Control** is the preferred mode of leadership. Spiritual abuse is going on. People are restricted by rules that have no biblical basis but do have a biblical façade. People are afraid to speak out or they will be excluded, or worse— called in by the leaders to be grilled and judged. When people leave, either a conspiracy of secrecy or public condemnation seems to cover their exit.

- **Guilt** is the preferred mode of motivation. Sermons end leaving the hearers feeling inadequate. Attenders are made to feel that unless they toe the official line, they are bad people.

- **Gossip** is the preferred mode of communication. People are put on notice through the circulating chit-chat that they are falling short of the church's glory. This allows people to be condemned without actually having done anything wrong, except in the eyes of those who think they have.

- **Downsizing** is the preferred mode of purity. No one who is caught in a sin is ever restored. While no one should be happy about sin in people's lives, the only tool this kind of community has to deal with sin is to toss out the offender.

Honestly, you will not receive much help in communities like these, if you are even willing to risk it. So what are you to do? Let me encourage you to find a spiritually healthy faith community to be part of, because you will never achieve spiritual healing alone. Why do I say never? Well, first because God did not mean for us to be alone. Even in the Garden, God saw that Adam was incomplete alone. God not only gave Himself to Adam, but He gave him the human companionship of Eve as well. In Jesus we have been given his community called the church where God's Word reveals that we have the opportunity to learn to love, serve, restore, encourage, live in harmony with, have fellowship with, and worship with one another. All are brought together because there is strength in this spiritual collective called the church. God saw we needed one another to reflect the glory of Christ, to spur one another on to become what we are created to be.

Second, to determine to go it alone is a pride decision. John Ortberg once said that pride is the only sin for which there is no 12-step program. It's that powerful. We make this kind of decision because it feels right without it being right. This is our sin speaking through our thoughts using our own voice. Secret-keeping is about what pride believes you know rather than acknowledging what God knows. Pride is saying that it knows better than God what you need for spiritual health. This cannot be true or you would have already become a healthy soul. The only thing isolation has done for you is to allow you to bury the hurts deep out of sight. Nothing has been done to heal the wounds or to free you from the sin. Pride would keep you there if you are willing to listen to it.

Why should you find community? Mainly because it keeps you from lying to yourself that you are okay when you are not. I fielded a recent call about a leader who had been caught in an affair with someone else's wife. He rejected a restoration process that was put together to help him renew his walk with God, and had been out of church for over a year. Now some friends were approaching him about being part of a leadership team of a new church start. He said he was ready, that his marriage was better than it had ever been. My caller asked me what he should think. Among other pieces of advice, I suggested he find out who else was saying this leader was spiritually healed besides himself. What this man needed from this new community was not a blank check, but a reality check. I encouraged the caller to sit down with him and tell him some truth in love.

Henri Nouwen warns us that "without community, we become individualistic and egocentric."[10] When we go it alone, we never really know if we are getting well. One of the reasons

God has placed us in community is precisely because of this inability. As lone rangers, we become a law to ourselves. Thus we can stonewall any challenge to our perspective about our spiritual health. But in community, we are given relationships where the truth about us can be tested and unfinished business can be ferreted out.

However, I have learned along the way that not every sibling I have in the church is safe. Giving up secret-keeping is not about spiritual voyeurism, letting people who do not fit Paul's descriptive in Galatians 6:1-2 gawk at my soul or revel in my bad choices. The people you and I need to help us to deal with our unfinished business are characterized as spiritually maturing, gentle (people with strength, but strength under God's control), humble enough to know the power of temptation, and so loving as to be willing to tell us the truth yet at the same time to share our burdens. These are the kinds of people who will not throw us out and dust off their hands in relief. These are the ones who are safe. There may be only one or two of them in your congregation, or a whole platoon of them. It is time you sought them out and entered into a deeper community with them.

You need this kind of community because you must receive certain things from others besides safety if you are going to stop being a secret-keeper. You want to find people who will care about you. But just because people care does not mean they will do you any good. You are looking for more than social acquaintances. To become your created self, you have to have deep spiritual friendships. Here are strengths you are looking for in such companions for your healing community.

- People who are absolutely convinced that God delights in them and you. And that He is truly working in all things (including your messy, wounded soul) to bring good in a way that will conform you to the image of His Son. People with a wrong view of God are not yet on the journey to become healthy.

- People who know what sin addiction is all about even though they may not share the same ones that have their grip on you. These people are able to be transparent about their own journey and to practice mercy instead of judgment. To these family members you can confess your sins without receiving judgment back in return.

- People who will not be afraid to tell you the truth gently, even rebuke you when you give yourself permission to continue in your addictive sin actions. They can see through excuses and rationalizing, but do not indulge in rule-making to straighten people out.

- People who will not give up praying for you without gossiping about you.

- People who are listening to God better than you are at the moment. They may be shown destructive aspects of you that you are overlooking because you are too close to see these things.

- People who will spur you on in a transformational pursuit of God. They cannot let you go on the way you have been.

WHERE YOU WILL FIND COMMUNITY

How will you find this level of fellowship within your faith community? Let me be really, really honest. There is no such thing as instant community. It will take you a huge investment of time and honesty to develop this kind of community. I do not mean 'time' in terms of the calendar, but of presence. You have to make time to be with others in your community a priority. To be available for the I-am-with-you moments—moments of in the pain or at the party—when being present matters. If you truly want real community instead of just social community, you will have to travel with people across the learning divide until you come trust each other with the worst as well as the best in you. Trust is a commodity that comes with walking through fire, rain, blood and mud together.

Honesty is the second key to community. Take off your self-protective mask. Be open to say "This is me, my weaknesses as well as my strengths." Ask God to stop your need for pretending to be the only person untouched by the Fall. In time you may find yourself ditching the victimhood, dropping the veil and transparently exposing your deepest needs to each other without anyone as much as raising an eyebrow. Maybe not the first night, but it will come. You need to pursue this community within your fellowship more than you know if you are going to have a safe one where you can stop being a secret-keeper.

If this reality doesn't scare you, then start with the people with whom you have genuine relationships. Ask if they and you can invest spiritually into each other. If you belong to a small group, time can and should be given in your meetings for spiritual accountability and input. If it is not, challenge the group to do so. Allow the time it will take for this group to become a deeper community before taking the step of secret-telling. You might also ask a mature person you know well, in whom you already see the Galatians 6:1-2 characteristics, to be your spiritual mentor and help start such a group.

Or start a small group study in the area of transformation and invite whoever is seeking the promised freedom in Christ. Focus on book studies that actually address with hope issues with which the people in the group struggle. Or you can join an existing group that addresses specific wounds, such as divorce or addiction, or loss of a child. You will find people there who are already open to you because you are on the same journey.

These are just suggestions. At the heart of finding community is the word "intentional." You will never have the depth of community you need accidentally. It cannot be one of your casual pursuits. Do not live for "someday" when people will just somehow automatically hang out with you. If you lack the people skills to build such relationships, ask someone to help you. But make sure you look for friendship above all other contributions that a faith community can make in your life, except for delighting in the Lord.

Choose carefully. You need people who are restorative— not a commiseration group. You will not be helped by people who feel sorry for you. You need people of understanding, people who have the honesty to know that, but for the grace of God, they would be in your shoes. Or people who have been in your shoes and are not afraid to own up. You want people who are bold enough to challenge you to know God and loving enough to keep your nose above water while you pursue intimacy so you can be healed. Finding this band of brothers (or sisters) takes time. Start investing your time in deepening relationships now. There are many ways open to you for this to happen.

One word of caution, however. Beware of the "leaven of the Pharisees." Do not open your soul to people who are wedded to the obedience model of spiritual maturity. They will condemn you in the end when obedience fails to rescue you. And afterwards you will find secret-keeping more entrenched in your life than ever.

CONFESSION, PRAYER, AND HEALING WORDS

In this healthy community you confess. Confession means taking a strong stand of accepting responsibility. "I chose this. I knew it was wrong. I rebelled. I hurt God and myself. My choice has now wounded others. I want help to know how to come back. How can I learn to know and trust God more? What does God need to heal in me? Who do I need to forgive?"

James instructs believers to "confess your sins to each other and pray for each other so that you may be healed. The prayer of a righteous person is powerful and effective" (James 5:16). This is the foundation of being made whole. Yet all our basic instincts rebel against such counsel. We are more prone to hide in plain sight, to hold back the part which reveals the worst aspect of our choices, to put the best spin on our sin that we can and hold on to our secrets. The sign that marks this path is "The Lie of Satan." He is at the bottom of encouraging you to stay silent about your *sin in me* choices. Why? Because he was a liar and a murderer from the first, Jesus said. Staying with his original plan, he is out to kill you dead emotionally, mentally and spiritually and he can accomplish this merely by convincing you to keep your mouth shut.

Secret-keeping is not the pathway to healing. Confession is. And confessing your sin to a community stocked with people who are neither shocked nor judgmental is what makes this so healing. I remember a guy coming to me and blurting out a deep secret sin that was destroying his life and marriage. He had never told anyone before and did not think if he did that he would tell a pastor. When he realized that I was not going to tell him off, throw him out or remind him of this again and again, he began to experience healing for the first time.

Being part of a community like this is healing. Making such a community is for those who are bold in their trust of God's healing process. They take James' direction seriously and bring it home to all who want to be free. I was told a story by a teacher who regularly coaches people in transformation how a man approached him after one of his talks, asking how he could have what the teacher had. This teacher invited him up to his room. Sitting him down, he looked him in the eye and said, "Confess to me three sins you have never told anyone else." The shocked man looked at him for a long minute and then blurted out three long standing issues he had been ashamed to tell anyone before. The teacher's response was, "Praise God! Do you want something to drink?" Again the man was startled and asked how the request for a drink fit into the conversation. Lovingly, the teacher told him that he himself was thirsty and, by the way, wasn't it great that the man could confess his sin without someone jumping all over him in judgment? Then the teacher prayed for him and he was really healed. This newly freed man went forward in his life telling others about his confession, how it released him from the addiction of sin and how they also could be set free by confessing their sins. This is what confessing sin in community will do for you as well.

Confession avoids the pitfalls of fad counseling. When we finally find a community where we can open our soul, we want someone to accept and understand us. Unfortunately, we also may want someone to mitigate our responsibility in what we have done, to tell us we are not at fault. Much fad counseling does just that.

Stores are full of books that offer various counseling approaches to help people. Many—not all—of these books tell people they are victims and, no matter what they did, they are not at fault. Television pipes these ideas right into people's homes with the glitz of celebrity endorsement. And then these counseling techniques find their way into the thinking of otherwise clearheaded people and come out of their mouths as pearls of wisdom. In our overly counseled society, the idea that pop psychology could be leading people just plain wrong is something we need to take seriously.

Countering fad counseling, confession says we accept the responsibility of our choices. It readies us to engage with God in the matters of our heart. We find we have to stop lying to ourselves when we confess. I remember a time when I risked confession with my co-workers. I had lied to a close friend about something. I remember I was trying to tell myself it was really nothing. So I was lying to myself as well. I knew I needed to confess this and ask those I ministered with to hold me accountable. The silence in the room and the shock on their faces is what I recall most as they absorbed the reality of someone they held in high esteem confessing broken neediness. But they rose to the moment and shepherded me towards reconciliation with the one I lied to and restoration in my walk with God.

All of us want to be the hero of our own story. We want to tell the past so it looks like we would have been okay if only the wickedness of others—much greater than our wickedness—had not invaded our world. We fought back. We did what we needed to do to survive. We were the victims. So our confessions can end up being weak and evasive, like the one I have heard so often as someone launches into his or her personal defense, "I know I am not perfect, but…" This is not confession. It's hero worship of the person I most want to protect—me! In saying such things I have just lied, and until I see this, I will not get well.

You have to stop blaming others for your choices. You have to own your part in how you came to have the stuck identity that is now eating your lunch. More than that, confession is essentially about secret-telling. Besides opening your heart to God, you are openly sharing about your life choices with others who have the opportunity to speak truth into your life. It may be painful truth, hard to hear, but in a healthy community truth always comes from people who really love you. They will win nothing if they squash you. Confessing to God before them can instead be cathartic. It allows your actions to be seen for what they are, and your wounds to be cared about while you heal.

The second thing you do in a healthy community is get prayed for. Although you probably will not have to ask for prayer, do not hesitate to do so. James indicated that confession and prayer are what people in community do for each other to hurry along the presence of forgiveness and health among themselves. To pray for someone is to recognize it is God, not the community, who heals. God already knows the secrets of your heart. Prayer by those to whom you entrusted your secrets acknowledges their trust that God will actually heal you in spite of however feeble your own faith is at the moment. And because of the empowering presence of the Spirit in each person, their prayers for you become powerful and effective.

Prayer for healing is much more than bringing a person's need to God's attention. It is specific. "God, your son (or daughter) is caught by his choice of _____ (specific sin). It is killing him. He cannot escape by his own power. Please, set him free from this sin and fill him with your grace, freedom and love as he surrenders to your leadership over his life." Believe me when I say that people who pray like this for you have had the same kind of prayer prayed over them at some time also.

When you ask for prayer, the elephant in the room is not just your *sin in me* choices. The rest of the story is the fact that someone wounded you and you need to forgive that person to be free. I watched a couple of leaders stand with their arms around a hurting woman and pray that God would give her the power to forgive the offender in that moment while they were praying. These leaders knew that without forgiving and releasing the offender, the woman's healing would lack depth and completeness.

Unforgiveness is a sin trap as much as any choice you will make in your life. When you are in community, remember that these people know what it is like to be wounded, since everyone you will ever meet is wounded. The people in your community who are praying for you are usually far along in their faith journey. They will know the challenge of forgiveness and the power God grants to those who ask to show mercy on those not deserving mercy. Ask them to pray that by God's grace you will release the debt of being wounded by another into His hands.

Community is where you also receive the gift of healing words. Jesus works through people to deliver healing words for our wounds, such as in 2 Corinthians 1:3-7, where Paul offers his readers comfort out of the comfort he has received from God. Comfort is not absolution for your destructive choices. Healing words are not given to affirm your victimhood. They point to the faithfulness of the One who powerfully heals your wounds as well as delivers you from *sin in me*'s grip.

Healing words are not platitudes either. These words are not about cheering you up with human encouragement, such as, "You'll be alright." or "Go ahead and cry. It will do you good." Healing words are instead strong reminders of *the reality of the gospel and God's presence in your life*. They point to the power and presence of God in your journey, statements like,

"God reigns over your life and He is using what has happened to further conform you into Jesus' likeness." And, "God loves you unconditionally and you will never be lost to Him." And, "God is your Shepherd. He will lead you through this dark valley and you will come out whole and healthy on the other side." And "God is your Father. No one will ever care for you like He does. He will heal you." And, "Peace! Be Still!"

There is a secondary benefit from this aspect of community. Healing words often disclose that these others have lived in the same dark corners you have inhabited and drunk the same bitter cup to the dregs as you did. You find you are not the only one in your group who has been addicted. What you feared when you told your secret may bond you deeper with the people you are in community with because you all know the bite of the same choice. The benefit is not that you feel better about yourself because they all failed too. The benefit is that they have passed on the hope-filled compassion of God to you that they experienced and now you all have comfort to share with anyone else who has wandered that same path. This is the sign of real humility within the community.

When you come to this point of real secret-telling, hope shows up. With God, there is no condemnation (Romans 8:1-4). He knew you could never be good without His grace. So confession is your path to the future, where you find release from your past choices and the hold your symptoms have had over your life. The addiction begins to lose its power over you.

This may seem incredible to you at this moment, because the addiction seems impossibly strong. But understand this—an addiction gains a greater hold over you when it is kept hidden. When you choose to no longer keep it a secret, you gain freedom.

You will find for yourself that God keeps His promises powerfully. He is faithful, and the past He will remember and cast up to you no more. Confession will bring you to the point where you will be able to let it go too, not to forget, but to be released from its power. Then you will be able to use its lessons at some future date to help another.

RESTORATION IN COMMUNITY

The fourth affirmation mentioned in the first chapter is all about why God put you into a faith community. One of the functions of a faith community is to restore broken people, not to beat them up in the process. Because everyone is wounded by living in a world full of people affected by the Fall, this has to be one of the most visible occupations of the church. Why visible? Because this is its witness to those outside the community—that salvation is not about being loved because one is good, but that one is loved while going through the messy business of being transformed. It is the gospel being demonstrated before their eyes. The good news is that no one gets lost again; that everyone will be restored to their created self by the power of the Spirit.

This function can be hard on those who are easily embarrassed. As individuals, we hate owning the mess others get themselves into, identifying with the sin people of our faith community practice, especially when it is tossed up in our face as typical behavior of "hypocrites." We want to disown such people and distance ourselves from them. Except that is not how it works in Jesus' Kingdom. Paul put it this way: "Carry each other's burdens" (Galatians 6:1-2). Now the place he wrote that was right in the context of restoring someone who had been caught in a sin. So it is not the burdens of nice, clean people in our faith community Paul is directing us to carry. It is the disorderly and rebellious whose burdens we are to share.

Some people might think that is not fair. Yet here's the rub. There is zero difference between those who have blown it and any of us. Their sins may be riper than ours at this moment, but those sins are no worse than the ones we may be living comfortably with. God forbid, but you or I may be the next who will need restoration. So take this to heart. If someone judges others rather than grapples with the task of restoring them, that person will find no one will be interested in helping with his or her restoration. If you carry other's burdens, you will find people to carry yours when you need it.

I bring this up because I know how unhappy people can be over sins that are not their own. And I think many are unhappy because they do not know how to help the person who is caught up in sin out there where everyone can see it. I mean, as long as it was a private affair and was not rocking anyone's world, live and let live. But now that it is front page news, instead of restoration, many in faith communities go into a damage control mode.

One real life newspaper story I found myself in involved a well-known believer. Barry was both a leader in a Christian organization and on staff at a large church. But then he got involved in a very public mess that landed him in jail and in the paper. He posted bail that day and tried to pick up his life as it had been. Except it didn't happen. The organization dismissed him immediately and the church would not even allow him to come to his office to clean out his desk. Barry found himself kicked to the curb by his church family and decidedly went into seclusion. For weeks he did not leave his house.

Some of his friends attended the faith community I was leading at the time. They came to me and asked if I would be unhappy if Barry just showed up on Sundays. What a question! I urged them to bring him. Then I and others in the community became involved in his restoration. This was no small task, and cost us much time and prayer. But that is what a faith community does. In the end, he was restored in his walk with God, in his marriage, and to those who at first rejected him. He went on to minister again in his field and continues to live before God as a man who has had people carry his burden.

Not all restoration processes turn out well. Some people choose to run until God chases them into the ground.

Sometimes in order to protect the well-being of others, the faith community has to practice exclusion until the person comes to his or her senses. People in the grip of addictions can do much damage to communities as well as themselves. This is always sad.

But protection is not about our reputation. God needs no protection nor does His name. A healthy faith community, which holds on to people at their worst, has to be willing to bear the reproach of people who do not understand grace and mercy. Their reward is to see someone who was lost being found, someone who was blind now seeing. I promise you, you will never get tired of this. It is truly amazing grace.

This is the beauty of belonging. You are never alone, especially when you need others to bear your secrets.

9. HOW YOU KNOW YOU ARE GROWING

YOUR JOURNEY HAS MARKERS TO MEASURE PROGRESS.

I sat in sorrow across from a man at a restaurant I'll refer to as Luke. I had met him several years before as part of a team that taught similar truths that I believe about unfinished business. I liked him as a person and enjoyed his partnership in seeing people pursuing healthy souls. He had taught a number of men about the need to recognize their heart issues and to draw close to God for healing. They listened to him and took their first steps towards freedom—except Luke did not go with them. Several of Luke's *hurt of the heart* issues remained so closed off that not even God was let in. Like so many others, he made *sin in me* choices that led to a damaging addiction to homosexuality.

We met that day at the request of his wife. Luke was openly living with another man. He knew this was a denial of all he believed. He knew he was hurting his wife and children by abandoning them. But he no longer could stand up against the pressure of his emotional pain and deny himself what he considered his need of this addictive relationship. Even as I urged him to yield to God's transformational power and His love for him, Luke looked this truth in the face and said, "No." This was not about his choice between his wife and the man. It was how he chose to answer Jesus' question, "Do you want to get well?"

I think of Luke as I write because Luke taught me a lesson I do not want to forget. Teaching transformation is not the same as experiencing transformation. I know a lot about soul health, about how God can and does change people from the inside out. I can point to people I have mentored who have taken these truths seriously and pursued a healing relationship with God. But if I hold back, neither all I know nor my telling others these truths will make me healthy. Information is not the path to becoming whole. I can nod my head and agree as did Luke that it's all true—and still crash and burn.

This raises a critical issue for all who desire to get well. We will be lured to our doom if we think mere knowledge of the *hurt of the heart* is enough. Or that simply having the knowledge of the *sin in me* will heal us. Possession of knowledge is not the cure. It really isn't the goal of the journey on which God has us. Knowledge of what is wrong can distract us from going on, from the pursuit of knowing God and being restored to wholeness.

To progress down the journey to wholeness, everything must be on the table, *regularly, continuously*. There can be no nook or cranny we know of in our soul that we can wall off, thinking it will not matter. Every time God opens our eyes to a *hurt of the heart* issue through His ruthless searching, we have another stage of transformation opened to us. We have the opportunity to learn a new level of humility, to admit again our inability to heal ourselves, and to receive God's grace. Not to do so is pride talking. We are saying "No" to God because we either believe we are the gatekeepers to what God is allowed to deal with in us, or that we are wise enough to deal with the pain in our own way. Both conclusions are the lies of the serpent from the Garden. Both lead us to miss the power of grace for, "God resists the proud, but gives grace to the humble" (1 Peter 5:5).

The story of Luke is not just a cautionary tale. It's reality. At whatever point I say "No" to Jesus' question is the point I not only stop going forward toward becoming whole, I actually start wandering backwards. In time, I will be living the damaged life again as I was before, although now it may be a different version. But I will not be on the road to becoming my created self. It will still be buried deeply under the unfinished business I chose to ignore.

The good news is that Luke's story is not over. I hope for the day to come when he chooses differently about his *hurt of the heart* issues and yields to God's healing. Not even a damaging choice is hopeless this side of the grave. Time is not a problem when it comes to grace. Some of you might think that it is too late for you. You might think that you have said "No" for too long and now age has caught up with you. You cannot become the *real you* now because you think you're excessively old. This too is an arrogant lie. Time and age offer no barrier to God's transformational work. *So what* if you are over sixty or approaching your eighties! God, who is from everlasting to everlasting, knew your name before He created the world. He purposed to transform you so that you'd be like Jesus. Only your well-aged pride will keep you from what He is willing to do in you even now in your twilight years. Don't let age be an excuse for missing the joy of becoming all you were created to be. The invitation to walk the journey towards spiritual wholeness is renewed every day.

HOW YOU KNOW YOU ARE ON THE RIGHT JOURNEY

As on all good journeys, markers are so vital for knowing how far you've traveled. I am writing this chapter at a retreat center near the Blue Ridge Parkway. If you want to get the most out of driving that scenic route, you need a guidebook that tells what you will find as you progress past various mileage markers. There are trails, waterfalls, and breathtaking vistas to see, as well as Appalachian culture preserved at rest stops along the way. The roadside markers keep you in touch with where you are and how far you have to go to reach a described destination.

Markers dot the progress of the journey you are taking with God as well. If "Yes" is the answer you give to Jesus' question each time, then you probably want to know that this choice has mattered. Is yielding to God's grace worth it? Are you getting well? How do you know you are transforming into the real you? What are the markers that indicate progress?

Jesus sat down on the top of a hill one day and, calling his followers closer in, began teaching them about what it meant to belong to the Kingdom. He started this talk with what we call the Beatitudes, referring to a series of blessings that Jesus declared were characteristics of those who were under his reign. Often people try to understand these statements separately, but they should be taken progressively instead. Rather than describing different aspects of Kingdom living, each blessing leads to the next, moving people towards a transformational goal. Not only does this approach make better sense of the Beatitudes, these then become our guidebook, identifying the markers of personal growth progress as we enter on the journey towards becoming whole. Each one shows us something about our personal progress.

HUMILITY: BLESSED ARE THE POOR IN SPIRIT, FOR THEIRS IS THE KINGDOM OF HEAVEN

The starting point of all healing begins with what I call "coming to the end of yourself"—the moment when you recognize that what you think are your resources and strength for health are actually totally inadequate. This Beatitude marks the death of pride in your personal resources to fix yourself. You cannot even start your journey towards becoming whole until this marker is passed. Until that instant you still vainly believe you can find some other way.

This is a marker of safety. To come to the end of yourself

is to belong. It is to receive the Kingdom life of Jesus for your own, to be granted access to the transformational power you personally lack. The sign of this is the presence of the Spirit in you. Every time you come to this point, your grasp of God's reign over you is renewed.

Do not be confused by the words "every time." This is not about needing to be saved from the penalty of sin over and over again. God reveals that justification (being freed from the *penalty* of sin) is a onetime deal. I refer here to being freed from the *power* of sin. This is the ongoing pursuit. The struggle for all of us is that we will need to come to the end of ourselves *every time we become aware of sin's control over our lives.*

Because God has already decided you will be conformed to Jesus' likeness, you will come to the moment where you will come to the end of yourself. You might come willingly or come kicking and screaming, but you will come to it. Perhaps you already know what I mean by this. God has allowed all your personal props to be kicked away, and what you have left in your possession gives you no relief from the pain. Or you are sick of your addiction and are begging for help from the only Being who could possibly release you. Or maybe you finally recognize you have been going through the same experience over and over—identical story, different faces, same outcome. A clone of the same jerk is working at this job also. The new spouse read the book the previous one wrote. You made a lateral move and found that the new place was exactly like the last. This reoccurring story is the one I know best because I've been there.

In some circles, this is called the "desert experience." The desert is often used in the Bible to depict a place of loss and grinding down. But it has a deeper meaning than merely punishment. Hosea records that God uses the desert as a place to restore His wayward bride, Israel, to wholeness, where He has isolated you to Himself (Hosea 2:1-20). God is not interested in beating you down. He intends to make you whole.

You may be going through a desert experience at this very moment. What you thought was your security is slipping away. What you used to comfort yourself is no longer up to the job. You may be extremely angry at God because of where you find yourself. Or afraid you are beyond hope. Or ready to cash in your chips altogether. The desert is worse in your eyes than the underlying *hurt of the heart* that led you here. Do not despair, no matter how hard things are. God is using the desert to bring you to a point of restoration. You are closer now to coming to the end of yourself than you have ever been.

For you who have grasped the need of humility, you know there is nothing to fear in placing yourself into God's hands. You may have suffered the loss of things that really offer no help. You may have lost face with people whose opinions you formerly valued. But what God has done in exchange is to bring you wholeness. You are beginning to live free as a child of God. This is the blessing of this first Beatitude.

The Fall has conditioned us to fight or flight in response to sin's power; the Beatitude shows us that the quicker we give up to God, the sooner we will be on the way to becoming whole. Stop and ask yourself, "How long does it take me to give in to God over heart issues?" As you heal, the speed of your surrender should increase as you learn to trust Him better. This is how you know that you are making progress on your journey.

GRIEVE: BLESSED ARE THOSE WHO MOURN, FOR THEY WILL BE COMFORTED

The second blessing speaks of grieving. When we come to the end of ourselves, we come face to face with wounds we have stuffed down, ignoring what we must do to really have a healthy soul, and doing that for as long as we have had the strength.

This blessing addresses one of the most profound aspects of the healing process. If humans are deficient in one area, it is their willingness to grieve properly. This denial of grief points to where we begin to run from pain, seeking comfort in something other than God. When we move towards knowing God, our pain becomes very alive and real. Here for perhaps the first time we mourn our loss, experiencing the intensity of our soul's distress. Grief is a process through which our rational mind comes to understand our emotional loss. We are freed to care that we are wounded, to stop denying that our wound is really significant or that we are really too big to cry. For the first time we can be safely real about the *hurt of the heart* issues. We can grieve how we messed up without an, "I told you so!" from God. We can even grieve wasting time taking this to God.

Grieving properly is hard because we keep getting stuck in one of the stages. Perhaps you bog down at stage one, denying something wounding happened and stuffing pain. Or you are parked at stage two, mad as hell and ready for revenge if you can figure out at whom to toss the lightning bolt—a parent, former friend, ex-spouse, that jerk of a boss, or even God. Maybe you are still in stage three, bargaining for a better ending, or stuck in stage-four, deep depression over what you cannot accept.

Possibly, as you read over these grief stages you think they all sound pretty unspiritual and you want to be above all that. You cannot, so don't mischaracterize the process. Instead, find yourself in the Psalms, where David and other writers recorded their own grief treks, sometimes in the middle of their hurt. Their inspired reflections may help you as you traverse your own grief journey.

Grief is not forever. Sorrow is not your permanent assignment. It leads you towards growth and health. Moreover Jesus, who understands loss and pain, is the one who will walk through the time of grief with you. You are never alone and without hope.

The promise of this grief process is not finding acceptance of the pain, but being comforted in a healing way. Wounds will never be acceptable. The blessing gives hope that, although the wounding was unfair and wrong, not only will every tear be dried someday, but also strength to live healed will now be given.

I heard the story of one woman who had been regularly molested by her uncle until she was old enough to leave her home town. She managed to avoid him for years by refusing to come to family gatherings. Depression haunted her until she finally sought help from someone who understood unfinished business. As she grew to know God, she wept many tears over the pain she had received from her uncle. As she healed, she recognized he would never stoop to apologize to her. She asked God for the strength to deal with this man. Surprising everyone, she attended the next family get-together. She waited until she could catch her uncle aside and spoke to him this way: "Uncle, both you and I know what you did to me. But I tell you right now that God has given me the power to forgive you for what you did. So I do forgive you and hope someday you can be changed from the kind of man you are." The uncle could not understand this mercy. It drove him towards God. For her it marked the shifting of the focus of her life from her wound to her God.

Being comforted does not mean you will have no scar from the wound. But it does mean the hurt of the wound no longer directs your life choices. Now you are free to move on differently from when you tried to fix it or deny it. You can move ahead trusting that God will use the wound in your life to conform you to the image of Jesus, even if you cannot see how at the moment.

SUBMISSION: BLESSED ARE THE MEEK, FOR THEY WILL INHERIT THE EARTH

Grieving opens your way to submitting to God's leadership in the healing process. The word "meek" literally means strength under control. To become meek is to agree that God is in charge of the program and you are willing to let Him set out the journey of your recovery.

There is no cookie-cutter process in God's program. This one truth probably bothers more people than anything else about God, and leads many to contest the process altogether. We would never say this out loud, but we prefer a predictable God with predictable steps we can understand and easily follow. This rarely is true of God's path. Healing may take you down roads that no one else has gone. He may ask you to do outrageous things—forgive people who do not deserve forgiveness, confess to others things you want to keep hidden, give away what you want to keep. No one can foretell what you personally will have to embrace on your journey, but here is the point. The more—and more quickly—you submit to whatever He reveals is for you, the more you know you are progressing. And whatever He leads you to do, He will also give you the strength to do it. This is where you abandon your self-help agenda and depend on God's grace.

The result of this choice is that all you have lost to the lies of wounded emotions will now be given to you. Inheriting the earth is to live life here as it was meant to be lived. You begin to come alive as a human. What was shriveled in your heart starts to bloom. You think differently. Your desires become wholesome. Your words become wise and insightful. What had become tasteless to you now regains its proper meaning in your life, whether it is your work, your family, your marriage, or your faith. You find that you are beginning to value the right things and hold casually those things that you used wrongly to define your life's significance. The growing submission of meekness indicates you are moving forward.

FOCUS: BLESSED ARE THOSE WHO HUNGER AND THIRST AFTER RIGHTEOUSNESS, FOR THEY WILL BE FILLED

What changes in you who choose this way is that you finally want to be what God made you to be in the beginning. You begin to want your life to reflect His life, perhaps for the first time, perhaps deeper than you ever thought possible. This blessing indicates that those who come this way have passed the point of passivity. They are no longer content to experience spirituality in passing. Their deepest necessity is to join with God in the active pursuit of letting all they are mirror His presence inside.

This pursuit is not just in the big things or in big ways. Again, transformation is not about better church attendance, more Bible reading, or giving lots of money to God. How God might go about shaping your religious life is not what this blessing is about. It is about the reality of the new covenant God promised in Jeremiah 31: 31ff—that He will put His law in our minds and write His law on our hearts. Then He will be our God and we will be His people. In other words, this blessing indicates our switch from selective obedience to passion for being righteous in the way God is righteous. It becomes a way of life in us. We want to look like our Creator. This is an amazing change for descendants of the couple who were convinced by a lie that they could do without God.

I learned how deeply satisfying this is a long time after I submitted myself to God at the start of my journey. I had always been critical of my wife, Shirley, since our marriage. I arrogantly found that she did not measure up to my standards of doing things—how she kept house, how she raised the children, etc. I foolishly sought to fix her through pointing out her faults, thinking that in time she would get better. I had no idea how badly I was wounding her and destroying our marriage.

One day, soon after I entered into the healing process with God, He showed me I was to stop criticizing Shirley. I was staggered, because my standard mode of speaking was to be critical and I knew nothing else. It sounded impossible to me. But because now I wanted what God wanted, I submitted willingly, asking that He do this in me by His grace. A year later, conditions had so changed in our marriage that Shirley, who journaled her thoughts, wrote in her notebook that day all the reasons she loved me as her husband. The first statement she wrote was, "I love Steve because he doesn't criticize me." I first saw this list seventeen years later, on a day when Shirley was cleaning out her storage chest. When she handed me the list, I was dumbstruck at the confirmation of God's changing our marriage by changing me years before. Through that one act of obedience love was rekindled in my wife. Do you think I was not filled that day? Even now the memory is a feast for me.

Look into yourself and ask what drives your desires. The healthier you are becoming, the greater you will find that you want what God wants. One of the sure signs you are making progress is that you look back at your former behavior and realize you never want to go back to what you were. That is marker number four.

COMPASSION: BLESSED ARE THE MERCIFUL, FOR THEY WILL RECEIVE MERCY

As you grow towards wanting what God wants, you will find yourself also growing in compassion. Nothing will open your heart to other wounded people more than realizing how you acted when you were comforting yourself by *sin in me* choices. You finally see their pain too. Whereas before you were selfish, you are now seeing other's wounds as being as important as your own.

There is a difference here in this Kingdom blessing. Lots of people care about those hurting, even in the midst of their own painful lives. Getting well is not an earthly prerequisite to compassionate activities. Lots of people go into the field of counseling damaged people because they themselves need counseling. Many go into the ministry no healthier than those they shepherd—not much job satisfaction comes out of this. There are many organizations advocating for the poor and oppressed that care nothing for this process. There is more to this blessing than compassion.

Instead, this blessing is rooted in the previously shared meaning of mercy. Mercy is not receiving the justice one so richly deserved. Merciful people are those who are not exacting retribution from those who have earned it. What you must see in what Jesus was saying about those who are being transformed is that, as they become like him, they begin to experience the same compassion for the people who wounded them that he demonstrated towards those who crucified him.

When I tell people who I am encouraging to launch out on this journey that one day they will be able to forgive those who hurt them, they either laugh or become angry. The last thing that will ever happen, in their minds, is that those responsible for their wounds would ever be pardoned. But this is a critical marker of progress. How do you know you are getting well? You begin to understand the wounded souls of the ones who made your life hellish. You realize they did to you what was done previously to them, maybe not in exactly the same way or intensity, but certainly resulting in the same kind of damage.

For example, nothing will change your attitude towards having compassion for the parents whom you may hold responsible for your *hurt of the heart* issues more completely than learning their history. Finding that your grandparents were also depraved may be a surprise to you! Or that your parents were traumatized by life may enlighten you towards the blessing of this Beatitude. This is about being able to give to others what you so truly need yourself from God.

CLARITY: BLESSED ARE THE PURE AT HEART, FOR THEY WILL SEE GOD

As you shed the grip that *sin in me* has had on you, the life of Jesus in you comes alive. You are now living life abundantly, as he promised. You start understanding that the *sin in me* choices have not only damaged your soul, they have made it impossible for you to know God as He is. Shame or defiance has marked your relationship with Him up to this point.

Instead of being blinded to God as the consequence of your unfinished business, the haze now is lifting. What has kept you away from God are the lies you have believed about Him. These lies have distorted God's beauty and approachability for you. You have not only failed to see Him as He is—Abba, Father—but you have questioned His trustworthiness and often assumed the worst about Him when you deigned to think of Him at all.

Purity opens our eyes to see that God is not like our human parents. Because we can only speak about God using human language, we all have the bent to interpret God through the filter of our human relationships. We put the kind of human face on God which reflects the brokenness of our own relationships. And then we blindly dance, not to God's tune, but to the tune of a god we have created. I recently heard an interview of a prominent believer in which she talked about growing up with a father from whom she had to earn love, so she saw God that way for years. I do not know your parental experiences. They may have been excellent or brutal, close or smothering, controlling or indifferent. Many *hurt of the heart* issues have their genesis in family home life. Accept this truth—much of what you have projected on God comes from this part of your past, and it keeps you from a relationship with God that is naked and unafraid.

As you have healed, all this has changed in you. As your soul is made well, you begin to see God as He is for the first time. The further you journey, the more you will come to know God better. His being will become clearer to you. Whatever forms the enemy's lies took for you now fail to deceive you as they did. God's will becomes your delight. His Word lights your journey. His purpose for you shifts from being a burden to a joyful occupation that you enter into with passion.

Your mind is also being refocused. This is what Paul speaks of in Romans 12:2 when he says, "Do not be conformed any longer to the pattern of this world, but be transformed by the renewing of your mind. Then you will be able to test and approve what God's will is—His good, pleasing and perfect will." You can see this is a transformational work. Renewing your mind so that you believe the truth about God— moreover, know God better—has to be done to you. You can never do it in your own strength. The more unfinished business you allow God to deal with in you, the more your eyes are opened to the true God who loves you no matter what. You will, as Paul says, then be able to put to the test His will for you and discover how appropriately good, pleasing and complete it is for your life.

This is how you know you are making progress, when you find that you have changed how you think and speak about God to others and how you speak to Him personally.

For example, your personal time with God changes. In the past you may have dreaded coming before God, expecting a recounting of your failures and sins by Him. Every time you prayed in the past, it was confession time and you abjectly groveled in repentance. But you cannot remember a time that you really enjoyed being with God. Or maybe your time with

God was a long recital of requests: bless Johnny, bless mother, do this, answer that. Your prayers were your duty and you popped in daily to make sure you could check that off your to do list. But there was little personal interaction to be found in these times. You were not sure your prayer got beyond the ceiling of the room. As you become pure in your heart, you discover prayer brings you peace and freedom in being with God. You open your heart to Him and experience His restorative presence without measure. That is the blessing of this Beatitude.

TRANSFORMATION: BLESSED ARE THE PEACEMAKERS, FOR THEY WILL BE CALLED THE SONS OF GOD

As a fully engaged Kingdom person, it is here that you are arriving at the purpose of God for your life. For this blessing is about how much your life has been conformed to the image of Jesus. To be a peacemaker is to be a bringer of *shalom* to others. *Shalom* is a word from the Hebrew that denotes wholeness in the presence of God. It is a gift from God and can only be received from God. To be a peacemaker is to be doing the work of Jesus, leading people back into a life-giving relationship with God.

Jesus is our peace, Paul reminds us in Ephesus 2:14. His life purpose was to bring an end to the disruption of God's relationship with man, to bring *shalom*, the hope that we could live a whole life. In turn, even before we received this life, God purposed to morph us to be like Jesus. It is then that we are truly revealed to be what we are—the sons of God. It is here that you know that you have been substantially healed. You can now fully see that what you have surrendered to God's hand had been holding you back from the real you.

Let no one who reads this shake your head and say it isn't true for you. Perhaps you are not very far down the journey towards this marker. You still see your life in terms of the grip that your *sin in me* choices have made. You are hard-bitten or remorseful or doubtful. Your destination is *not* determined by your present state. It is *predetermined by God*. Since He has planned this for you, it will come to pass as you surrender yourself to His process.

How can you tell you are progressing in this direction? Let me point to the one characteristic of God that appears in those whose lives are conforming to Jesus'. They become lovers. Emotionally, mentally, and spiritually they act out of love towards others, as they now know love in ways forgotten by the human race in its mad pursuit of doing what it prefers. In fact, the mark of growing health in someone's soul is that one's love for God and others increases as time goes by.

Frankly, when you get to this place, you not only love differently, you also begin to grieve for people who have not allowed themselves to know God's love because of their choices. You look around and see people you know who have the same opportunity to get well as you did, but are making the choice to not deal with their unfinished business. You envision them whole and desire *shalom* for them. And so you proclaim the good news of peace to them, in hope that they will take the same journey you did, finding some will and others won't. Your world becomes a bitter-sweet place.

Love costs. It cost you pride. You discover that as a peacemaker you gain a greater awareness of the pain you passed on to others. You cannot let it pass anymore. You will more readily pursue reconciliation with those you hurt. The time between wounding and repenting will become shorter and shorter as you grow in love. Wholeness is worth it, because you are now becoming part of those who rescue, rather than those who inflict. This is when you know you have reached this marker.

PERSECUTION: BLESSED ARE THOSE WHO ARE PERSECUTED BECAUSE OF RIGHTEOUSNESS, FOR THEIRS IS THE KINGDOM OF HEAVEN

This concluding Beatitude may cause some confusion, since I suggested that Jesus was teaching these blessings as a series progressing towards a goal. It may appear that the peacemaker Beatitude makes a fitting end to the journey. But Kingdom living is rooted in reality, not idealism. Putting this another way, when Jesus got to the end of his journey, there was a cross waiting for him.

When you seriously deal with your unfinished business, you will find you are making unexpected enemies. People who once loved to hang out with you suddenly see you in an unfavorable light. They may verbalize their new disdain for what you are becoming, calling you names or spreading hurtful rumors about you. Personal attacks may be the order of the day. Even physical threats may come.

Travis was one such person. Years in the drug culture had given him a personal community he related to while using and whom he met again in the twelve-step program rooms. As long as his life paralleled their lives, all was good. Then he began to pursue a living relationship with God. As he experienced transformation over time, his former friends began to make fun of him, upset that he was no longer interested in living on the merry-go-round of using and getting clean, with its accompanying lifestyle. When he asked me why this was happening, I pointed out Peter's warning: "For you have spent enough time in the past doing what pagans choose to do...They think it strange that you do not plunge with them into the same flood of dissipation and they heap abuse on you" (1 Peter 4:3-4). It took him some time to come to grips with what was happening in his social circle.

Yet to do justice to Jesus' teaching, it is not just the people who are outside the Kingdom of whom he is speaking. Religious people can be the source of abuse as well. Why is this? Well, for one reason, people are hiding their own stuff. They react badly to those whose pursuit of healing might suggest judgment on their status quo way of living out the faith. Others are using Christianity to attain some kind of social position or power, so the transformational process can be very revealing of their duplicity. Besides, the enemy is always seeking to stir up trouble. Change in one's life with God offers loads of opportunities for Satan to create misunderstandings and plant accusations of spiritual one-upmanship in the minds of others who should know better.

This may be troubling to you when it happens, but never be surprised by it. Jesus experienced it too and laid out your response. "Father, forgive them, for they do not know what they are doing" (Luke 23:34). You'll have to practice this numerous times before you are home with the Father. Be ready.

Do not assume that you will finish this journey, as in someday you will be done and can move on to other things. These blessings mark a lifelong journey. You are invited by Jesus to walk through this way continually, as over each *hurt of the heart* issue he asks the question, "Do you want to get well?" The longer you are in the process, the more you see your need to be transformed. Happily, God does not reveal all our brokenness in one setting. If He did, we would be so devastated that we would never ask God for the courage to go on. But as I tell people, every morning I see myself in the mirror and I know I have not yet become like Jesus. And neither have you. God, however, is committed to moving us forward, and that is enough to quell the fear.

Because we are on a lifelong journey of going from brokenness to wholeness, we will see these markers again and again. God will show us what we need to address at the right moment. Each time we say "Yes," a new stage of growth process begins. We will tread past the markers continually as we deal with our unfinished business throughout our lives and move towards becoming healthy souls.

10. GOING ON WITH YOUR JOURNEY

I recently taught at a church that had hosted me a number of months before. That first time, a young man had rushed forward in response to the question, "Do you want to get well?" He had been living with lies so long that they were his life. He had been stuck waiting for God to somehow free him. This time he came up to me to let me know he was moving forward in freedom. The relaxed joy on his face was in total contrast to the first time I saw him. I know he will find support in his faith community because it is full of people who are also on a journey with God.

The prospect of guiding people towards a transformational journey gets me up every morning. So perhaps the saddest aspect of offering unfinished business counsel is when people do not move on in a journey with God. They are extremely interested in the teaching. They really do enjoy learning the principles. "Eye-opening!" some put it. But they are not going anywhere. A year later I might come back into their world to find them running in place, with a new language to explain their place, but with no forward motion.

This is opposite to the world of Jesus. He said to the man by the pool of Bethesda, "Take up your bed and walk," and down the road the man went. In Jesus' Kingdom, people are healed in real time, souls are knit back together, and sin loses its addictive power. People get to walk—to leap, frolic, skip, hop, spring, gambol, and experience forward motion in their spiritual, emotional, and mental lives by every movement word in the thesaurus. In other words, standing still is also your choice, but it does not have to be your destiny—or your destination.

TAKE UP YOUR MAT

So, *do you want to get well*? Jesus is inviting you to chuck your stuck identity, take up your mat, and walk. This invitation from Jesus answers a question I often get asked. The person asking usually is trying to process transformational ideas for the first time. And so he or she might ask some form of the following: "If God is the one who does the changing in me, am I supposed to just do nothing at all, just sit like a pawn and wait for Him to move me forward?" To answer this, I have to be clear on an important distinction. There is a difference between *magic* and *faith*.

Under the sheen of religion, people confuse miracles with magic. Magic, in its truest sense, is about the work of power on an object. The object has no say in whether it should be manipulated. In magic, objects are merely passive and are changed or used regardless of their desire to be or not. Not so the miracle. Miracles require a faith response from the people involved. Miracles are joint ventures, so to speak.

People who approach God as if He is a divine magician

look for Him to abracadabra them into restoration while they watch. The trick Jesus pulled at the Bethesda pool—"That was pure magic."—is their way of seeing it. God-does-it-all-we-do-nothing is not really what this story tells us. It never is about a man passively being magically healed. Yes, there is Jesus' display of divine power, and it is unequalled by any trick performed by Penn and Teller. But where the story hangs on tenterhooks is whether or not the man would actually pick up his mat.

Engaging in the transformational process is a lot like physical exercise. Picture a room full of overweight, out-of-shape people listening to a talk on the importance of exercising. Then they watch some DVDs on how to exercise, followed by a few minutes of practicing some simple forms of exercise. Would you be surprised if all these people in the room were still unfit a year later? Physical fitness does not happen when someone understands the theory of working out. People become fit through engaging in consistent, regular exercise. And people become transformed when they by faith act on what they are offered by Jesus.

Jesus is not offering us a magical solution to the symptoms we have. He is offering us restoration and health. But you have to pick up your mat. You have to say "Yes" to the offer. You have to come to a point of faith in which you will respond to the command to get up rather than thinking it may be true, that you would love to see it be true, and someday it may come true. Passively waiting for God to do more while you watch is the same as saying "No." Faith is saying, "Okay, if you tell me to do this, I will trust that you will actually keep me on my feet and give me the strength to walk home with this mat in my hands."—and then seeing Him do just that.

Responding in faith to the question does not mean you will automatically "feel" safe or even that your damaged emotions will no longer fight you for control of this decision. Damaged emotions are dedicated to the hopeless quest of finding a safe place in the world away from your pain. Even though you agreed with your damaged emotions to make a *sin in me* choice as your safety harbor—a choice you may now see as devastatingly injurious—you are still going to run all alternate choices through the gauntlet of these same emotions. Your damaged emotions are familiar, they seem to tell you truth— but they cannot be trusted! They have already led you into dark places, why would you trust them now? You have to get a grip on this reality and firmly remind yourself of it every time your emotions scream for you to stick to the destructive course.

Picking up your mat means you trust God's offer for real healing. That act of faith can be upsetting, uncomfortable, inconvenient. But you will have to choose it to get to where you really want to go. And then you will have to continue to trust God, since faith walking is always harder than it looks from the sidelines—because we are more damaged than we realize.

One of the people I watched learn to trust God over her emotions was a single mother of three. The wounds of her life were found in the lack of love and dignity she experienced growing up. When she began learning how to trust God with her unfinished business, she was tremendously encouraged. So she picked up her mat. But the roots of the wounds went deep and so, every week at the small group we were in together, she would come with a new complaint of how hard life was and how unhappy she was. I finally asked her if she only felt normal when she had a crisis to share. That brought her up short. She began to realize how much she was letting her emotions continue to speak for her. Slowly, she allowed God to heal and rein them back into their proper boundaries. She has gone on to a fruitful life with a husband who loves her deeply.

So what should you do? The first thing is to ask God to show you what He wants you to do. What form does His invitation to pick up your mat take? Does He want you to stop swearing? Do acts of kindness to people that you do not like? Be generous even when you face bills of your own? Stop complaining? Apologize to someone you wounded? Be at peace over a personal flaw or disability you cannot change? Give up an addictive behavior you still get pleasure out of? Confess infidelity? Forgive the perpetrator? Or, like me, stop criticizing your wife? Ask God and He will provide you with the road map by which He will take you to health. And ask Him to help you distinguish His voice from the voices of your damaged emotions so that you know this is the right mat to pick up.

I discovered on my own journey the necessity of asking God to help me distinguish His voice because I was to ready to substitute my voice for His when it came to asking where my symptoms were coming from. I was wrong every time I depended on my own best thoughts and stayed by the pool much longer than I had to when my voice overrode truth I needed to get well. How do you know you are hearing God's voice? Here are four benchmarks that have guided me. First, I know I am hearing God because what I hear is a revelation about myself, often a totally new thought that was not in my repertoire of self-talk. I have heard these from God when I stopped doing all the talking and listened. But that is not all. The second benchmark is when I have an emotional resonance with this new truth. It does not merely sound convincing or convicting, but the new truth touched the deepest part of my soul when I heard it.

This leads to the third benchmark. When I heard this revelation, I experienced a sense of hope instead of despair. This is how I know it is from God and not Satan. The enemy knows truth about me too. However, when Satan speaks truth into my ear, I feel defeated and exposed. When God speaks, He speaks as a Father, a Daddy who loves His child and wants me to be whole, even if the path to wholeness is through the pain of facing what and who has wounded me and knowing how deeply sin has saturated me. Revelation from God causes me to be assured I will come out in the end picking up my mat and walking.

The final benchmark is an amazing one. I know that I have heard a revelation from God because it always leads me to a desire to practice forgiveness. And I mean both forgiving the one who caused the *hurt of my heart* as well as accepting God's forgiveness for me because I chose the *sin in me* to comfort that wound. You might think the first kind of forgiveness would be plenty enough. It is great to let go of a debt I have been holding against another wounded human being. But I always have found the second kind of forgiveness as necessary as it is harder. Necessary because the enemy would steal all the joy out of my life for being unable to do what only God can do in me. Forgiving myself is really only accepting what God has done. Not accepting forgiveness for myself embraces a sneaking lie that I still owe God something. Revelation tells me I am done with the past way of living and that includes owning a guilt debt already paid for by the cross.

Then you should do whatever God shows you. It may not at this moment seem sensible to you. "This is going to kill me to do it," you think. You may be saying you are not able to do what God wants. You would be right. You cannot. But He can. This is what grace is all about. You need to say to God, "I will respond to what you show me, but you will have to show up with power or I can never do it." His promise of grace means that He will show up as you by faith take up your mat. This is the stuff of appropriation.

But what God does not promise is that every mat-carrying scenario will lead to a happily-ever-after moment. Because He has an eternal perspective and knows everything from first to last, He may ask you to do some things that result in failure from your point of view. You won't see an earthly reward for your faith act. Underline that. Your children will still not appreciate your sacrifice for them. You may never master that skill you lack. People will not apologize. You will not get a job promotion. The divorce will stay final. You will still be plagued with health issues. Like Paul, the thorn in the flesh will remain. Understand that God is not asking you to trust Him for the right-in-your-eyes result. He is asking you to trust Him— period.

If you do, what you will get is contentment, because you will come to see that God has everything right concerning your restoration in His hands. So whether you are in need or have plenty, hungry or well fed, you will find you can do everything you need to do through His strength (Philippians 4:11-13).

At a deeper level, taking up your mat means you will open the door for God to enter the secret regions of your heart. If He asks to see your darkest secrets, to examine your most painful memories, to heal the unhealable as well as to reign over the addictions that own you, you say "Yes." You may not fully understand the implications of the question "Do you want to get well?" But in the end it doesn't matter. You will discover God is safe. And He invites you to pursue intimacy with Him so that you can know this for yourself.

A Faith Journey

Dealing with unfinished business is not merely to make you feel better. It is about you living out your life with God. It is about freedom and discovering how to fill your role in the Kingdom. "For God is working in you, giving you *the desire and the power* to do what pleases Him" (Philippians 2:13, NLT) Paul asserts. The endgame of your existence is to not only transform your character into the character of Jesus, but to live the life of Jesus daily by God's power in the community where He has placed you. This is what you were unable to do when your unfinished business was dominating your life.

If you have come this far in reading this book, and are pursuing greater intimacy with God than ever before, you have come to the end of the beginning. Dealing with unfinished business is not your destination any more than the airport you land on a trip is where you set out to go. An airport is a passing-through point to get you to where you are meant to go. If you have spent any time trapped in an airport waiting area due to delays, you know how frustrating not being able to get to where you want to go is. Now imagine if you had to spend days instead of hours waiting for your next flight. You would come out of that experience either a basket case or dedicated to dismantling that airline! Addressing unfinished business can be like that if you handle it like it's the goal of the journey instead of a temporary stopover. Instead of freeing it becomes frustrating.

You have to go on to appreciate the freedom God provides. To not go on is like holding the winning ticket to a fabulous prize but never cashing it in. So boldly go on to becoming like Jesus. Your next steps on this journey will be to add to your faith by engaging in training in righteousness. Let me unpack that sentence for you.

What does "adding to your faith" mean? The gospel focuses on a righteousness that is continually revealed in you as you exercise faith from the start of your journey to the last day you draw a breath (Romans 1:12). You have to exercise faith every day in this journey. You might be wondering how much faith you need to go forward with God. Well, how much faith did you have on the first day, the day when God moved you from death to life, from the Kingdom of darkness into Jesus' Kingdom? Wasn't that pretty powerful faith? That is the same faith you will need daily for this journey.

Adding to your faith is about gaining confidence in God along the way as He remakes your life. Compare this with a teacher or coach you might have known in your past. When you first met that person, you may have had no idea what he or she would do with your personal development. You may have even resisted some of the training exercises laid out for you because of your lack of understanding. But as time passed, you began to see the unexpected in yourself. The hidden abilities, the undeveloped talent that had always been there were brought out and put on display. As a result, you became that teacher's or coach's biggest admirer and found yourself telling others how that person changed your life.

Now suppose this teacher or coach also could give you the power to do what you always wanted to do—power beyond anything you knew you ever could be capable of? What if you saw him walking on the lake and you asked if you could join him—and you did! How much confidence would you have in this person then?

That is what adding to your faith is all about. Peter tells us that through our experience with God, we discover that He has given us all the power we need for life and godliness. Our confidence grows in Him as we see good stuff coming out of us that we never knew was possible. We can add to our faith such things as goodness, knowledge, self-control, perseverance, godliness, brotherly kindness, and love (2 Peter 1:3-7). He could have probably added more to the list, but you get his drift. Adding to your faith is always about "onward ho!" on our journey with God. The results make us find we want to brag on God.

Mind you, this is not an easy road. It's marked by warfare. And our own damaged emotions will try to drive us into the ditch. Some days will be tough on the journey. But an added-to-faith will keep you going on the bad days. If you know the story of Stephen in Acts 6-7, you catch something of what I mean. For Stephen, the worst day of his life was also his best. Even while people were taking his life from him, Jesus shows up to sustain him. And he will do that on your worst days too.

If you do not go on, you will get bored with Jesus in time. Peter's way of putting this is that adding to your faith keeps you from being unproductive and ineffective in your experiential knowing of Jesus (2 Peter 1:8-9). This is where the "training in righteousness" comes in. When you started, you were just a plebe, a raw recruit who did not know how to stand or which end of faith to hold onto. But as you go further on your faith journey and gain confidence in God, you no longer will be satisfied to stumble along. You will become eager to go on—to learn the drill—to be all that you can be.

Training in righteousness (2 Timothy 3:16) is a shorthand Paul used to express the idea of progressive education in the ways of God. This is where the "do" disciplines come in. As you are gaining intimacy with God through the "done" disciplines, so now you are empowered to live the life with increasing freedom and insight into God's thinking. The "do" disciplines you can pick from include study of the Scripture, prayer, fasting, service, celebration, and sacrifice. There are disciplines of abstinence where you choose to stop and root something out of your life that you have depended on instead of God. And there are disciplines of engagement, in which you seek to build the right kind of attitudes that guide your life with God. Both of these types of disciplines lead to deeper enjoyment of God. They teach you to be more dependent on His grace and teach you that He is bigger than you, which you probably say you know already, but do not really believe at the depth you will as you become more intimate with Him.

They also lead to discovering His purpose for you in His Kingdom. Going on is about personal faith, not private faith. This is not just another experience to add to your collection. You are being transformed to be like Jesus so that you can impact the world around you. You are surrounded by people caught by the same unfinished business that was sucking the life out of you. You now have good news to tell them. You have no reason to fear telling them because it is possible your personal journey will give them hope that God is and that He rewards people who go looking for Him.

In being conformed to Jesus' likeness, you also get to do Jesus' mission. "As the Father has sent me, so I am sending you," is the way Jesus put it. He said this to the motley crew we now call the apostles. They also had unfinished business in their lives. But they had the Spirit in them. Jesus was not telling them—or us, for that matter—that you will go on with my mission when you have it all together. God uses broken and messy people all the time to accomplish His work in this world. He will use you even while you are on your faith journey to be transformed.

This journey to wholeness will be your lifelong pursuit. Every day you will get to start fresh. Do not worry that your yesterday experience with unfinished business did not go well. Keep your eyes on God. Choose to draw near to Him in intimacy today. Take the faith steps He has placed before you. You *have* enough faith for today.

So take up your mat and go on.

END NOTES

[1] Nina W. Brown, *Children of the Self-Absorbed* (Oakland, CA: New Harbinger Publications, 2008), 19.

[2] Bill Gillham, *Lifetime Guarantee* (Eugene, OR: Harvest House Publishers, 1993), 10.

[3] David Benner, *The Gift of Being Yourself* (Downers Grove: InterVarsity Press, 2004), 58.

[4] I.D.E. Thomas, *A Puritan Treasury of Quotations*, (Carlisle, PA: Banner of Truth, 2000), 224.

[5] Jeff VanVonderan, *Soul Repair: Rebuilding Your Spiritual Life* (Downers Grove: InterVarsity Press, 2008), 65.

[6] David Benner, *The Gift of Being Yourself* (Downers Grove: InterVarsity Press, 2004), 63.

[7] Mike Yaconelli, *Messy Spirituality* (Grand Rapids: Zondervan, 2007), 13.

[8] Miles Stanford, *Principles of Spiritual Growth* (Lincoln: Back to the Bible Broadcast, 1972), 41.

[9] Gerald May, *Addiction and Grace* (San Francisco: HarperSanFrancisco, 1988), 122-123.

[10] Henri Nouwen, Michael J. Christensen and, Rebecca J. Laird *Spiritual Formation*: *Following the Movements of the Spirit* (New York: HarperOne, 2010), xxvi.

APPENDIX: HURT OF THE HEART INVENTORY

"An inside look is important, but ... it is tricky. The same Bible that instructs us to guard our heart (Proverbs 4:23) also tells us our heart is impossible to understand as well as deceitfully wicked (Jeremiah 17:9). The command to keep watch over our unknowable heart seems rather like ordering a guard to never let an invisible prisoner out of his sight. Clearly, if our insides are as difficult to know as the Bible indicates, then any hope of an accurate inward look depends entirely on God's willingness to help. Students of the human personality can uncover mounds of data and organize their findings into intriguing and perhaps insightful theories, but without God's help, no effort to explore the heart will ever pinpoint the core problems that need changing. The good news, of course, is that the opposite is also true. With God's help, we can understand what needs to be understood."

—Larry Crabb: *Inside Out*

The purpose of this inventory is to help you process with God how you have been wounded by others who have been affected by the Fall. This inventory does not contain an exhaustive list of possible reasons for the hurt of the heart; allow God to lead you by His Spirit towards what He wants you to know. To make use of this inventory:

- Choose to get alone with God apart from distractions such as your cell phone and computer.

- Ask God to show you which past experience is affecting you currently. Your hurt may be related to one of the categories, but will probably be connected with a specific person's actions or attitude or an incident in your life. Ask God to show you which past experience is affecting you currently. Your hurt may be related to one of the categories, but will probably be connected with a specific person's actions or attitude or an incident in your life. Ask for clarity from God. It is not what the hurt is itself, but what this hurt means to you. In what ways has it affected you?

- Ask how you may be seeking to comfort yourself apart from His real comfort.

- Ask God to show you that He suffered with you through your pain and has never abandoned you or given up on you. If you need to, ask someone to you trust to discuss the list with you.

BE WILLING TO BE QUIET IN GOD'S PRESENCE

UNTIL YOU KNOW YOU ARE FINISHED WITH THIS

PROCESS.

HURTS

- ☐ Emotional abandonment (ignored)
- ☐ Abuse (sexual, physical, mental or emotional)
- ☐ Harsh, unredemptive criticism (ridicule)
- ☐ Trauma (physical, mental or emotional)
- ☐ Loss through death or divorce
- ☐ Loss through bad decisions
- ☐ Rejection of your person or your best performance
- ☐ Unjust punishment
- ☐ Demands of perfection
- ☐ Made to feel that you do not matter
- ☐ Owning the pain of another person close to you
- ☐ No physical affection
- ☐ Neglect (deprived of the basic needs for food/shelter/clothing/security)
- ☐ Overindulgence
- ☐ Overprotection
- ☐ No investment of time
- ☐ Broken promises or being lied to
- ☐ Manipulation (being jerked around emotionally)
- ☐ Taught harmful values (hate/fear/ "life should be fair"/ "the world owes me a living"/certain kinds of people are inferior)
- ☐ Being bullied
- ☐ Hurts inflicted by your addictions (self-inflicted wounds)

REFLECT

1. During this time of being with God, which hurt of the heart did He draw you to from your past needing to be healed?

2. How does this hurt translate into your life—in what ways are you affected by it?

3. What do you believe are your next steps with God in healing?

4. What do you think you need to share with your spiritual mentor or community?

ADDITIONAL RESOURCES

BOOKS:

Backus, William. *What Your Counselor Never Told You.* Minneapolis: BethanyHouse, 2000.

Barton, Ruth Haley. *Invitation to Solitude and Silence.* Downers Grove: InterVarsity Press, 2010.

Benner, David. *The Gift of Being Yourself.* Downers Grove: InterVarsity Press, 2004.

Brown, Steve. *Scandalous Freedom.* West Monroe, LA: Howard Publishing Co., 2004.

Clinton, Tim and Gary Sibcy. *Attachments:Why You Love, Feel and Act the Way You Do.* Brentwood, TN: Integrity Publishers, 2002.

Crabb, Larry. *Inside Out.* Colorado Springs: NavPress, 2007.

Crabb, Larry. *Soul Talk.* Brentwood, TN: Integrity Publishers, 2005.

Curtis, Brent and John Eldridge. *The Sacred Romance: Drawing Closer to the Heart of God.* Nashville: Thomas Nelson, 1997.

Eldridge, John. *Waking the Dead: The Glory of a Heart Fully Alive.* Nashville: Thomas Nelson, 2006.

George, Bob. *Growing in Grace: When Giving It All You've Got Still Isn't Enough.* Eugene, OR: Harvest House Publishers, 1997.

Gillham, Bill. *Lifetime Guarantee: Making Your Christian Life Work and What to Do When It Doesn't.* Eugene, OR: Harvest House Publishers, 2012.

Lane, Timothy and Paul Tripp. *How People Change.* Greensboro, NC: New Growth Press, 2006.

Mabray, John T. *The Seven Deadly Sins and Spiritual Transformation.* Xulon Press, 2010.

May, Gerald G., M.D. *Addiction & Grace: Love and Spirituality in the Healing of Addictions.* New York: HarperCollins Publishers, 1988.

Nee, Watchman. *Sit, Walk, Stand: The Process of Christian Maturity.* Fort Washington, PA: Christian Literature Crusade, 2009.

Sandford, John Loren and Paula Sandford. *Transforming the Inner Man: God's Powerful Principles for Inner Healing and Lasting Life Change.* Lake Mary, FL: Charisma House, 2007.

Sandford, John Loren and Paula Sandford. *Letting Go of Your Past: Take Control of Your Future by Addressing the Habits, Hurts, and Attitudes that Remain from Previous Relationships.* Lake Mary, FL: Charisma House, 2008.

Sandford, John Loren and Paula Sandford. *God's Power to Change: Healing the Wounded Spirit.* Lake Mary, FL: Charisma House, 2007.

Scazzero, Peter. *Daily Office: Remembering God's Presence Throughout the Day: Begin the Journey.* Willow Creek Assoctiation, 2009.

Scazzero, Peter. *Emotionally Healthy Church: A Strategy for Discipleship that Actually Works.* Grand Rapids: Zondervan, 2010.

Scazzero, Peter. *Emotionally Healthy Spirituality: Unleash a Revolution in Your Life in Christ.* Nashville: Thomas Nelson, 2011.

Smith, Malcolm. *The Power of the Blood Covenant.* Tulsa: Harrison House, 2006.

TerKeurst, Lysa. *Made to Crave: Satisfying Your Deepest Desire with God, Not Food.* Grand Rapids: Zondervan, 2010.

Tozer, A. W. *Knowledge of the Holy: The Attributes of God: Their Meaning in the Christian Life.* New York: HarperCollins Publishers, 2009.

Trumbell, Charles. *Victory in Christ.* Peabody, MA: Multinomah Books, 2005.

VanVonderan, Jeff. *Soul Repair: Rebuilding Your Spiritual Life.* Downers Grove: InterVarsity Press, 2008.

Willard, Dallas. *The Divine Conspiracy: Rediscovering Our Hidden Life in God.* New York: HarperCollins Publishers, 1998.

Willard, Dallas. *Renovation of the Heart Putting on the Character of Christ.* Colorado Springs: NavPress, 2002.

Willard, Dallas and Don Simpson. *Revolution of Character: Discovering Christ's Pattern for Spiritual Transformation.* Colorado Springs: NavPress, 2005.

Wilson, Sandra. *Hurt People Hurt People: Hope and Healing for Yourself and Your Relationships.* Grand Rapids: Discovery House, 2001.

Wilson, Sandra. *Into Abba's Arms.* Wheaton: Tyndale House Publishers, Inc., 1998.

WEBSITES:

www.settingcaptivesfree.com (free online Bible studies and support for people with all kinds of addictions including gambling, self injury, overeating, pornography, drugs, drinking, etc.)

www.lifetime.org (further teaching on transformation by Bill Gillham)

www.abbafather.com (healing in the area of manhood issues by Gordon Dalbey)

www.transformingcenter.org (Ruth Haley Barton site that focuses on strengthening the souls of pastors, Christian leaders, and the congregations and organizations they serve)

www.TransformLead.com. (Ford Taylor is a transformational teacher and consultant for business leaders)

www.gracenotebook.com/pub/2.html (*But How*, by David Tryon — great little free article on the subject of transformation)

FOR MORE INFORMATION AND FURTHER HELP
PLEASE VISIT
DR. STEVE SMITH'S WEBSITE AT:
http://www.ChurchEquippers.com

Want to see what deadly sins are

affecting your life?

Visit

www.ChurchEquippers.com/KTDCResources/

for your free Deadly Sin Inventory.

For additional tools, please visit:

www.ChurchEquippers.com

61639989R00139

Made in the USA
Lexington, KY
15 March 2017